Failing to Figure

For Solveig and Richard —
epitomies of Bjørnson's 'Live in Truth'

Failing to Figure

Whitehall's costly neglect of statistical reasoning

Mervyn Stone

With a Foreword by

Dennis V. Lindley

Civitas: Institute for the Study of Civil Society
London

First Published May 2009

77 Great Peter Street
London SW1P 2EZ
Civitas is a registered charity (no. 1085494)
and a company limited by guarantee, registered in
England and Wales (no. 04023541)

email: books@civitas.org.uk

ISBN 978-1-906837-07-5

Independence: Civitas: Institute for the Study of Civil Society is a registered educational charity (No. 1085494) and a company limited by guarantee (No. 04023541). Civitas is financed from a variety of private sources to avoid over-reliance on any single or small group of donors.

All publications are independently refereed. All the Institute's publications seek to further its objective of promoting the advancement of learning. The views expressed are those of the authors, not of the Institute.

Typeset by
Civitas

Printed in Great Britain by
The Cromwell Press Group
Trowbridge, Wiltshire

Contents

Acknowledgements

The author wishes to thank Joan Davis, chairman of North West London's Community Voice, for introducing him to scandal number one and Jane Galbraith for professional help in exposing it. Dr Rex Galbraith of UCL kindly did the graphic. Dr David Green, Director of Civitas, generously allowed me to develop some of the material as pieces for the Statistics Corner of the Civitas website. The provocative indifference of others has been a continuing impetus, but not as much as the kind encouragement of leading statistician Professor Dennis Lindley. It was good to have expressions of support from civil servants who must be nameless.

Author

Mervyn Stone is an emeritus professor of statistics at University College London where he has been teacher, researcher and statistical adviser since 1968—before that, at the universities of Cambridge, Princeton, Aberystwyth, Michigan and Durham. He has been associate editor and trustee of Biometrika, editor of the methodology journal of the Royal Statistical Society and a member of its executive committee. His academic work—in the theory of experimental design, formal Bayes methods, large deviations, cross-validation, coordinate-free estimation and in a wide range of applications of statistical reasoning from psychology to stem cells—has appeared in over 100 papers and in *Coordinate-Free Multivariable Statistics,* Oxford Science Publications, 1987.

For the last two decades, his work has embraced issues of public concern—water privatisation, changing clocks to save lives, attempts to measure the efficiency of police forces and universities, daytime vehicle lights, speed cameras, cycling accidents, NHS decision procedures and primary care trust funding. For the latter, he gave written and oral evidence to the House of Commons Health Committee inquiry into NHS deficits. Recently the tenor of his work has become openly critical, as in pieces published in the Statistics Corner of Civitas and in Civitas's immigration portfolio.

Foreword

All of us, in a modest way, have to decide how to spend what we earn; to balance our housing needs against education and the pleasures of entertainment. Also we need to judge whether work done for us was effective, and what future demands are likely to be. Governments have problems of a similar nature on a much larger scale. In this booklet, Mervyn Stone discusses six problems encountered recently by English governments, concluding that the methodology used and the results obtained were unsatisfactory. The allocation of money within the NHS is complicated, without rational basis and probably inefficient. The knowledge about our water supply is inadequate. The assessment of how well the police do their job is questionable. The effectiveness of speed cameras is open to doubt and the statistics of immigration were, and perhaps still are, wrong. Perhaps weirdest of all is the determination of grants from central government to local authorities. Finally, after the discussion of broad principles, Professor Stone makes several modest, yet potentially effective, suggestions that could be quickly implemented—and which should improve substantially the machinery of government.

One obvious defect in the present system is its lack of transparency, expressed in the desire of ministers and civil servants to keep matters confidential. In the allocation of money to primary care trusts, it is absurd that the statistical thinking for the formula that was eventually used has never been fully revealed to parliament and public. Had it been, people could have made constructive suggestions, for example concerning what data the formula might have used. Should mortality be age-standardised rather than the actual death rates? How should the demands of fertility treatment or obesity be compared with those of cancer treatment with expensive drugs? It is valuable to have the point of policy here openly stated. All the parties involved should remember that there is very often someone out there who knows more, or has better ideas, than they do. Wide dissemination is healthy, only marred by the clatter of cranks and the expenditure of additional time. One can appreciate that secrecy makes life easier—but secrecy is not usually rewarding in the end.

I urge all those involved with the consequences of governmental actions to read this book for its clinical analysis of six projects, and for its practical suggestions for improvement, both at a broad level and for immediate application. Some may feel there is a statistical bias in the analysis. If so, they are correct but should then ask what is the art and science of statistics? It is the study of uncertainty and its removal or reduction by the sensible use of relevant data. The government policy-making machinery is beset by uncertainty and must depend on data. Hence the apparent bias in favour of what has to be an ingredient in the making of most policy decisions.

Let me conclude this foreword by introducing a personal note. In my early research work, I had made what appeared to be an innocuous assumption and the results, both theoretical and practical, that sprang from it appeared sound. Stone came along and pointed out that the assumption was unsound. He provided an ingenious counter-example, where the assumption led to transparent nonsense. This upset me greatly and for days I struggled to find a flaw in his work. Reluctantly I came to the conclusion that there was none: he was right and I was wrong. My results needed amendment but it was found that, with the assumption modified to take account of the counter-example and the principle it involved, the new results were better than the old. It is the Wokingham counter-example that uncovered the flaw in Stone's sixth example—the Revenue

Support Grant formula. The main idea of this original and important book is that reforming the flaws in departmental machinery may remove the need for such counter-examples.

Dennis V. Lindley

Introduction

What's the problem?

For a good number of years now, England has been dominated by a handful of politicians with executive power over those at the top of the government's departmental hierarchies. The combined power of these politicians and their special advisers is increasingly misused to sideline honesty and truth in policy-making by exploiting or ignoring the deficiencies of the contractual machinery through which external expertise can be enrolled to assist policy-makers struggling with areas beyond their competence. The problem is how to remedy those deficiencies in a scientific fashion.

At the heart of the problem is a powerful and largely unchallenged convention: a minister sitting at the top of his departmental pyramid[1] can put a blanket of confidentiality over all the advice he or she gets from policy-making civil servants within the department (arguably reasonable[2]) and from *any advisory committee set up by the minister* (more than questionable). The advice of the committee is based, often very tenuously, on research commissioned by the committee and paid for out of the public purse. The documentation of that research may be liberally posted on the departmental web-site or even printed officially. What the claim to confidentiality permits is that the internal thinking and argument of the advisory committee can and usually does remain a closely guarded secret. The committee typically approves the specification of the research to be done, the selection of the research group that gets the contract from the field of those invited to tender, and then frames its advice in the light or darkness of the completed research. The icing on the policy-making cake is that the minister goes on to claim that the policy (sometimes a formula for the distribution of huge sums of public money) is based on authoritative and independent advice.

This book will add its evidence-based support to the voice of many others that this is a recipe for poor government—and then go on to explore ideas for doing things better. In 2007, the editor of *Computer Weekly* asked 'Will door stay shut on NHS secrets?'[3] He knew all about the sad fate of billion-costly IT projects—the quality of which can easily match the grosser examples in this book. There is a pressing need for some reduction in the pyramidal hierarchy[4] and a reconstruction of the departmental contractual machinery that enrols external expertise in order to subject policy-making to genuinely independent scrutiny.

Contractual machinery for soft science

There has been a misuse or failure of so-called 'soft' science—the sort of scientific activity that is associated with the organisation and management of complex systems and that typically depends on the expertise of economists, mathematicians, statisticians, system analysts and computer scientists.[5] Its administration differs substantially from that of the 'hard' science that studies physical, non-social, non-political reality. An important difference between hard and soft science is in the time-scale over which the consequences of failure become apparent.

The Challenger disaster of 1986 for the space agency NASA showed very quickly what may happen when a hard science is ignored: the space shuttle came crashing down when its 'O-ring seals' failed. The physicist Richard Feynman demonstrated the neglected science of those seals to an investigatory committee.[6] Later, he observed that:

> reality must take precedence over public relations, for nature cannot be fooled.

For England's Department of the Environment, Food and Rural Affairs (DEFRA), the cause of the foot-and-mouth outbreak in 2007 was found to be in particularly down-to-earth soft science—the failure of administrators to look after the drains of the laboratories of the renowned Institute of Animal Health.

Above ground, foot-and-mouth science is far from the kind of science that Keith Joseph had in mind when he insisted that the word Science be taken out of Social Science Research Council, changing the name to Economics & Social Research Council. The change showed that Keith Joseph's target was what he saw as the scientific pretensions of economics and sociology. It is, however, not necessary to say that there is no science in those disciplines to see that the science that they do have is of a different order. Within the typical time horizon of public policy, economists and sociologists are rarely exposed to the sort of reality test that killed the Challenger astronauts—unless they venture to make bold and testable short-term claims.[7]

Soft science involves the kind of scientific research that helps to ensure effective implementation of particular public policies or projects. It is the kind of science that government departments are currently able to take control of, by direct tendering and contracting to agents whose expertise is taken to exceed what is available within those departments. As such, it has become an important component of the machinery of government. But there is a yet-unresolved paradox in its widespread use by departmental hierarchies. Where does a government department get the competence to specify, manage and effectively implement any scientific research that needs to be done when, as the shape of the contractual machinery reveals, the department openly concedes that it is not competent to do the research on its own?

This book will suggest how the paradox can be designed out of the machinery of government. Sadly for Britain, soft scientific research has failed, time and time again, to achieve its objectives. The recurrent sickness has an aetiology that is intimately associated with statutory procedures that, by embracing secrecy, fail to register subversion of the scientific quality of contracted research in both content and presentation. It is my thesis, based on the evidence of the six policy-making examples exhibited in this book, that the administrative machinery is, to use a voguish term, dysfunctional—and that there is a pressing need for root-and-branch reconstruction.

My travels through lands on both sides of departmental boundaries have verged on the surreal:

I dreamt that somehow I had come
To dwell in Topsy-Turveydom!...
Where right is wrong and wrong is right
Where white is black and black is white.[8]

It seems almost that here are irrational forces working together. In reality, it is more helpful to suppose that policy-making failure is avoidable cock-up rather than conspiracy to subvert rationality. There may be, here and there, thoughtless error or even concealment of deliberate deception, but there are too many participants in the usual fiasco to allege conspiratorial con as a driving factor. So, when we come across another illustration of topsy-turveydom, we should suppose (in the absence of evidence to the contrary) that things have 'just grown'. Growth without an evidential or rational basis can produce monsters. There are hugely expensive funding formulas in my first and last scandals that Topsy's response to Eva in *Uncle Tom's Cabin*[9] fits like a glove:

EVA: *Do you know who made you?*
TOPSY: *I s'pect I just growed.*

1

Kill or Cure by Formula in a Statistical Playground

Inside the black box—a snake!

For 2008/09, National Health Service (NHS) providers got £74 billion from the 152 primary care trusts (PCTs) that now cover England. Each PCT gets a slice of a national cake. Its size is determined by a formula proudly introduced by Health Secretary Alan Milburn in 2002:

> The resources are being distributed according to a new fairer funding formula. Poverty and deprivation cause excess morbidity and mortality. They bring extra costs to local health services. The new formula reflects those costs by using better measures of deprivation and by taking greater account of unmet health needs. The new funding formula is fair to all parts of the country.[1]

As I write this in 2008, another Health Secretary, Alan Johnson, is on the BBC's *Today* programme introducing a 'chance in a lifetime' reformation of NHS England on its 60th birthday. It is to be based on a 'bottom up' plan by minister Professor Lord Ara Darzi who has already pronounced (in his plan for London) on the matter of 'under-doctored' areas that Johnson is highlighting. In the section 'From deception to delusion' below, I explain how the formula has been used in a way that biases the true picture of the way GPs are geographically spaced.

It is a formula that produces large inequity in the level of funding. Some PCTs get twice as much as others per head of the populations for which they are responsible—and these are large populations of hundreds of thousands. By 2007, the House of Commons Health Committee was gearing up to investigate whether that inequity could be one cause of the large deficits that a significant proportion of the then 303 PCTs were running into. Writing in the *British Medical Journal* under the headline 'Time to face up to "scandal" of funding formula', the then health editor of *The Times*, Nigel Hawkes, gave forceful expression to his intuition:

> Sometimes it is the unasked political questions that are the most interesting. If a political party stood up before an election and said: 'We intend to give some areas of the country twice as much money to run their health services as others', questions might well be raised. The obvious one would be: 'How on earth do you justify that?'. [2]

A Civitas press release in January 2006 was headed 'Another Explanation for NHS Deficits: The NHS Formula for Dividing 60 Billion Based on Faith not Science'. This was to advertise a Statistics Corner piece in which I had tried to explain, for a wider readership, the provenance and structure of the formula and its possible causal relationship to at least some PCT deficits. The piece ended with constructive suggestions of how the machinery of government should handle disagreement among 'experts'. It was a privilege to get an unsolicited response from the Director of Policy for the NHS Confederation:

> I am not a statistician but I understand enough of your paper for it to have caused me very serious concern about the resource allocation process. I have tended to regard it as a **black box** commissioned from independent experts and I had largely missed the AREA work despite being a policy specialist—it was kept very quiet inside the NHS and as far as I was concerned there was none of the discussion that accompanied the York formula in 1993/4—which included peer-reviewed publication. Reading your paper has brought it home to me how little was discussed in public. ... You are quite wrong to say that governments have a problem when experts disagree—on the contrary except in matters which can be falsified later they have a significant opportunity to pick and mix their advice which is precisely what you are saying here! [My emphasis]

The Target Index formula from 2003 to 2006

Target Index =
0.8276 × Hospital & Community Health Services (HCHS) index +
0.1407 × Prescribing index + 0.0250 × General medical services index +
0.0067 × HIV/AIDS index, where HCHS Index = {Age-profile index ×
Additional-needs index × Market forces factor (MFF) index ×
Emergency ambulance cost adjustment (EACA) index},[3]
where Additional-needs index =
0.8553 ×
{0.008 × Education deprivation index + 0.013 × {Proportion of low birth-weight babies} + 0.070 × {Standardised mortality ratio for under-75s} + 0.026 × {Proportion of over-75s living alone} + 0.108 × {Standardised birth ratio} + 0.103 × Income deprivation index + 0.225 × 1st Morbidity proxy index + 0.548 × 2nd Morbidity proxy index + 0.375 × 3rd Morbidity proxy index + Adjusting constant}[4]
+ 0.1447 ×
{0.358 × {Comparative mortality factor for under-65s} + 0.338 × {Proportion of over-60s claiming income support} + 0.034 × Housing deprivation index 0.636 × 4th Morbidity proxy index + Adjusting constant},
where Age-profile index =
{£591 × number of under 5s + £225 × number of 5-14s + £445 × number of 15-44s + £532 × number of 45-64s + £966 × number of 65-74s + £1584 × number of 75-84s + £2358 × number of over-85s},
and where
1st morbidity proxy (for nervous system disease costs) is based on age, sex and the two percentages of university 'participants' and attendance allowance claimants over 60,
2nd morbidity proxy (for circulatory disease) is based on age, sex and the three percentages of university participants, non-whites, and invalidity benefit or severe disability allowance claimants,
3rd morbidity proxy (for musculo-skeletal disease) is based on age, sex, the two percentages of non-whites and under-65s with limiting long-term illness and on the health deprivation index,
4th morbidity proxy (for psycho-social disease) is based on age, sex, the two percentages of non-whites and under-75s with limiting long-term illness and on the income deprivation index.

The use of mathematical formulae to influence the way money for health care is allocated goes back to Richard Crossman, who authorised what can now only be described as a mouse of a formula. It varied from region to region with *population* (weighted for age and sex profiles), *bed numbers* (weighted by speciality costs) and *case numbers* (weighted by national costs).[5] Move on 40 years and the box shows where Nigel Hawkes's 'twice as much' came from. Mr Milburn's new formula was more snake than mouse—but still a completely man-made artefact. The snake is a translation into well-nigh verbal mathematics, for readers of this book, of the 18 pages[6] that the Department of Health (DoH) used to explain the calculation in 2003 of a PCT's *weighted population* that can be carried out once all the basic input variables have been given their numerical values. The *target* allocation is the product of two numbers: (i) what the PCT allocation would have been if it were simply proportional to the actual (strictly speaking estimated) population for which the PCT is responsible and (ii) the *ratio* of the weighted population of the PCT (what DoH calls the *unified* weighted population) to the actual population. The first number corresponds to 'equality' of the notional allocation to individuals; the second number is what I here call the PCT's *Target Index.* It is the quantity that might be expected to have some rational justification for its introduction of inequality of allocation between individuals in different PCTs—but it is a statistic that was not listed among the spreadsheets of the DoH 'exposition books'.[7]

In 2006, Andrew George MP wanted to know the 'financial impact'[8] of each of the factors represented in the formula. Minister Burnham told his presumably frustrated questioner that it was not possible to state the financial impact of each adjustment in the formula—which is, er, not exactly true. My Figure 2.1 (p. 9) provides insight into the impact of factors when they are sequentially incorporated into the formula in the order in which they were incorporated in DoH's worked examples. At each stage of the sequence, the figure plots a *partial* index which is the value the target index would have if all the factors not yet incorporated were given the same national average value for every PCT (thereby excluding their influence at that stage). For Tower Hamlets and Wokingham, the different pattern of those impacts is why one of these two PCTs ended up with a Target Index of 1.50 for 2003/04—precisely twice the 0.75 of the other.

Figure 2.1: Two Ways of Hitting the Target

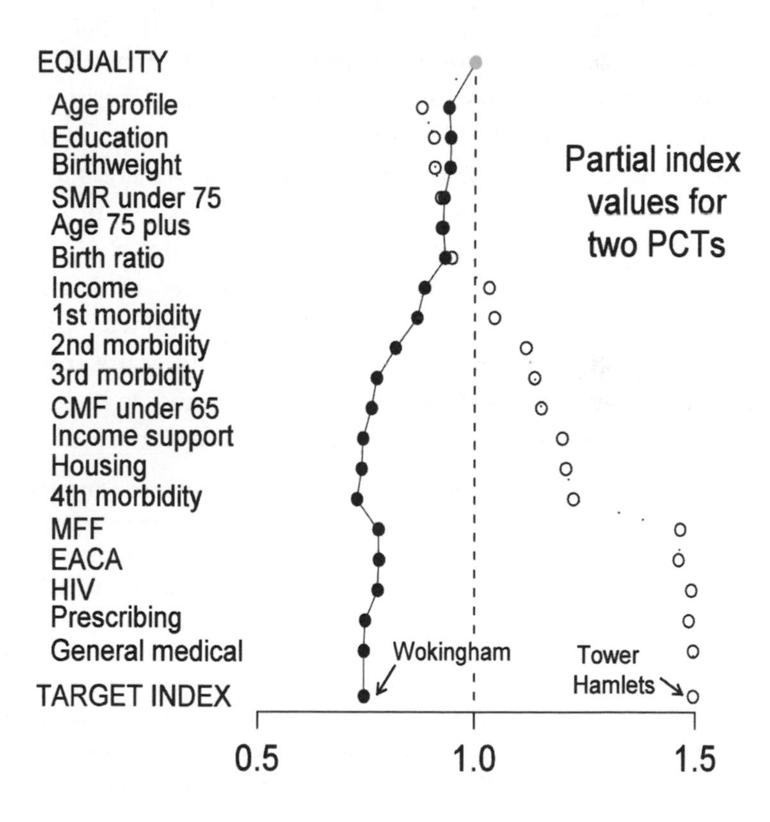

The wrong question!

In 2006, the House of Commons Health Committee opened its inquiry into NHS Deficits with questions to two chief executives and two finance directors. The chairman was Kevin Barron MP who, within minutes, was asking a superficially simple question:

> Is the funding formula used to allocate resources to PCTs fair?[9]

It might have led to more fruitful responses if the question had been about the *provenance* of the formula:

> Is there any rational basis for the way the formula has been made to depart from *equality*—giving every PCT population the same *per capita* allocation?

As it was, the question of 'fairness' did not carry a health warning about the significant problem of the definition of fairness itself. The NHS mantra is that it should provide 'equal access to care for those in equal need' which is a fine principle—if it were ever seriously entertained! In practice, difficult value judgements have to be made about the relative priorities in the allocation of resources to different sorts of health care. The question of fairness was posed repeatedly throughout the inquiry—but to little effect. Secretary of State Patricia Hewitt was obliged to face the question at the end of her oral evidence to the Committee:

> **Q721**. Almost everywhere I go around the country and in almost every group of parliamentary colleagues I meet, people complain to me about the funding formula... I have already asked the Advisory Committee to review the formula... so that it can inform the funding allocations for the next round, from April 2008, but I have to say, Chairman, and I really want to stress this point, all this argument about [the] funding formula is in my view a complete distraction from the need to sort out the problem now, because, whatever is right or wrong with the funding formula, we are not going to reopen the allocations for the current year and next year.[10]

Other witnesses were equally uncertain: the formula was 'as fair as anything else around' or 'a complex piece of work' or else 'whichever formula we have had to date there has always been controversy about whether it adequately reflects diversity or rurality', and so on. The fact is that simply looking at the formula does not tell us whether it is fair or not—even if we have a fair idea of what 'fair' means! Changing 'fair' to 'about right' appears to ease the problem of judgement. LSE professor and Number 10 special adviser Julian Le Grand may be one of those who think the formula is 'about right', as he revealed in a Civitas presentation[11] about education. A member of his audience suggested that any education voucher would have to be based on a complex weighted formula, which elicited the speaker's opinion of the already-operational complex PCT funding formula—that it was acceptable for the formula to be adjusted to look right. Another LSE professor, Simon Stevens (a health policy adviser to Number 10 and now employed by United Health, America's biggest health insurer), has said that academic studies (which he did not identify) have failed to show that the NHS deficits problem is fundamentally a resourcing problem.[12] Stevens must be one of the 'about right' school—whose adherents are somehow able to compare the funding figures with what they know about the individual healthcare needs of all those PCTs and then give a stamp of approval to the formula's black box that outputs the funding figures from socio-economic proxy inputs.

The 'about right' view may be expressing honest approval of the inequalities in *per capita* funding that were built into the formula with the politically-dictated aim of removing 'health inequality' (i.e the appreciable differences in standard measures of public health between the populations served by different PCTs). Approval of the 'about right' sort calls for a personal assessment of the ultimate efficacy of different funding levels in the reduction of inequalities in public health. These assessments are typically made without informed reference to the provenance or structure of the formula itself. They can only be based on a memory-taxing assessment of the *per capita* allocations and healthcare needs of individual PCTs. One has to wonder why, if there is any consensual validity in such assessments, there has been no attempt to coordinate them to determine resource allocation directly—without recourse to what most statisticians would see as statistical legerdemain bordering on witchcraft.

How the formula was fabricated

In the end, the formula was constructed by DoH as a do-it-yourself assembly using component expressions from academic suppliers. In the late Nineties, a research contract for a new funding formula for England to match New Labour's 'pace of change' was awarded to a team of health economists—academics subcontracted by the consultancy service of NHS Scotland's Information and Statistics Division (ISD). They were led by University of Glasgow researchers and can be conveniently described as the 'Glasgow team'. In 2003 when their work was done, Liam Fox MP[13] asked health minister John Hutton to publish the new but not yet operational PCT-funding formula. Hutton promised it would be published—but he misled Fox when he said that the ISD report[14] of the work of the Glasgow team was 'research into the new formula'. The team's achievement had actually been to stir several statistical-computing cauldrons and extract numbers that determined the shape of half-a-dozen mathematical expressions. But these were no more than potential components for the formula-to-be and they did not in any sense determine its final shape.

The expressions were passed to DoH's Finance Division in Leeds, who selected the two they wanted as building blocks in final assembly of the national formula for its roll-out in 2003. The report of the eight-strong Glasgow team shows that these expressions were not even among those that the team had recommended with any degree of warmth! They are the bolds and the italics in our snake (p. 7). With a permuted authorship, the team published a peer-reviewed account[15] of their approach with conclusions that were no firmer than tentative suggestions and that were illustrated by the derivation of just one of the expressions that DoH Leeds had rejected. There was then nothing in the research literature about the new formula until 2006.[16]

The remit for ISD had posed several challenges devised by DoH's advisory committee on resource allocation (ACRA). One challenge was for remedial attention to two core indices in the existing funding formula—the ones for age-profile and additional-needs. Another assigned task was to look at the possibility of their replacement by a single index before incorporation into an index for Hospital and Community Health Services (HCHS)—a possibility that the Glasgow team was unable to achieve.[17] But the most challenging request concerned the thorny question of 'unmet need' among poor and ethnic minority communities. The team gave that question a dusty answer—which seems to have been ignored by Alan Milburn when he told MPs in 2002 that the new formula was 'taking greater account of unmet health needs' than the formula it was replacing, in which 'unmet need' had no role at all! Four years later, Patricia Hewitt was assuring the Health Committee that the formula had been built to accommodate the 'very specific issue that some populations... do not make good use of the Health Service'.

The model-based expressions sent to Leeds were constructed from socio-economic variables acting as proxies for direct measurement of healthcare needs. Statistical games were played with the empirical relationship between many such variables and the existing utilisations (costs) of health services for patients in over 8,000 electoral wards covering the whole of England. The idea was that econometric theory could use statistical modelling to remove any 'supply' biases in those costs and deliver plausible and unbiased estimates of different sorts of healthcare need in individual wards.

Where did the Glasgow team get the nerve to start constructing its range of utilisation models? The answer must lie in the confidence that some econometricians have in *many-variables least-squares-fitted linear models* and the *subjective choice and judgement* that such modelling inevitably entails. It is a reliance dictated by necessity. Computerised linear modelling is the only feasible widely-taught statistical methodology for *empirical data ransacking*—selecting from a large collection of potentially explanatory variables those that may be judged to express a reasonably true relationship.

Linear models can be useful in science as representations of reality—especially when the ranges of variation of the explanatory variables are known to be so small that any possible curvature of the true underlying relationship can be neglected. When the German mathematician Gauss discovered the method of least-squares estimation at the end of the eighteenth century, it was for an effectively true linear model for geodetic survey data, that took more than adequate account of the Earth's curvature. But most scientific applications of least-squares linear modelling do not have such stringent adherence to the concept of truth. Linear modelling is used in exploratory data analysis as the structural support for broad descriptions of how the variation in a quantity of interest can be broken down into components that can be tentatively attributed to particular explanatory variables, leaving 'unexplained' residuals that do not get any such attribution. Linear models can *identify* interesting relationships and *indicate* the lines of future observational or experimental research. Experimentation may then be able to add causal inference to the descriptive picture.

It was least-squares linear modelling and associated subjective judgements that selected the two models for the snake's bolds and italics—with computing software whose misuse in recent decades would have had Gauss protesting from his grave were that possible. For both of the models involved, the unexplained residuals were a large part of the variation of costs between electoral wards—leaving plenty of room for equally plausible models with very different financial consequences. This issue surfaced in a Royal Statistical Society discussion paper in 2001[18] when Harvey Goldstein suggested that, since formulae based on uncertain modelling were 'fallible' devices, 30 per cent of funding should be set aside as partial insurance against failure. His suggestion ignored the reassuring statement in the tabled paper that such a proposal by a 'Conservative administration' had already been rejected by the government's own 'advisers and independent referees'. Peter Smith has raised the ante in an influential book[19] revealing that he expects government to accept assurances of technical experts that they have been careful not to let their subjective judgements be influenced by the allocatory consequences of any new formula.

One of the most emphatic statements in the Health Committee's report was an indirect comment on the subjective linear modelling judgements in the construction of the formula, that:

> the judgements made have a direct effect on the level of funds that are allocated to PCTs.[20]

Flies on walls are not yet electronically miniaturisable. We may have to wait years for an account of the lively discussions that must have engaged various bodies in and around DoH, when the Glasgow team came up with their recommendations. The only positive recommendations were for three statistical models of the utilisations of services that can be labelled: Acute, Acute + Maternity and Acute + Maternity + Mental where the plus signs mean that costs are aggregated prior to modelling. These models were rejected by DoH in favour of two exploratory models in which the Glasgow team had incorporated 'morbidity' indices in an attempt to satisfy the remit to think about unmet need—and these were the models for the snake's bolds and italics. A decision must have been made somewhere to ignore the explicit reservation that accompanied Glasgow's lukewarm recommendations:

> Given the time constraints and other aims of the project, our analysis has been *essentially exploratory* but in view of the *promising results* obtained **we recommend that further work on augmenting the set of needs indices be undertaken.** The immediate implications for resource allocation depend on the view taken about the robustness of the new morbidity indices. [My italics, Glasgow's bolds][21]

This is more caveat than recommendation. In effect, DoH was warned that *research* models based on morbidity indices should not yet be taken very seriously. That did not stop DoH using them to compensate for unmet need—by censoring variables with the 'wrong signs' that were taken to express unmet need. Any confidence the Glasgow team had in their own complex justification of positive discrimination by censoring was for models rejected by DoH. So the snake's bolds and the italics do not even get the underpinning that the Glasgow team was prepared to give to its preferred models—and even that underpinning would have been dependent on faith that linear modelling and subjective judgement can reveal the truth about healthcare need.

From deception to delusion

The formula's departure from equal national *per capita* funding comes from replacing actual[22] PCT populations by weighted populations, adding up to the same national total. If the distinction between a weighted and an actual population is blurred, the formula can be party to deception —as it was in 2005 and 2007.

In 2005, North-West London's Community Voice was addressed by chief executive Dr Goodier of the then Strategic Health Authority (SHA) for North West London. One of his Power-Point slides was boldly headed NWL SPENDS MORE ON HEALTH CARE THAN OTHER SHAs. North West London was at the top of a list of decreasing numbers (one for each of England's 28 SHAs) with a value of 114.9, whereas North East London was at the bottom with a lower value of 97.5. How did Dr Goodier's audience interpret those numbers? The clearly intended message of the slide was that users of NHS services in NW London should consider themselves very lucky—to be better funded than much poorer areas of London. That must have come as a surprise to most of the audience—residents of Hillingdon whose PCT in NW London's SHA then had the largest deficit in the country. The figures were in fact expenditures (in millions) per *weighted* population (in 100,000s). If Dr Goodier had used actual instead of weighted populations, NW London's luck would have come down from an 18 per cent lead to a much less impressive four per cent—and if he had broken the figures down to PCTs, his Hillingdon audience would have seen percentage inequalities of the sort that offended Nigel Hawkes's intuition.

In 2007, Professor Sir Ara Darzi published his plan for NHS London. The report[23] emphasised the sadly striking reduction in the expectation of life in individual London boroughs as you travel east from Westminster on the Jubilee line. But it used SHAs not boroughs when it looked at funding of 'health inputs' rather than 'outcomes' such as life expectancy:

> At the same time as there are big inequalities in outcomes, there is great disparity in health inputs, such as *funding per person*.[24]

How many readers of the report realised that its 'funding per person' figures were of the Goodier sort, leaving the others to be deceived into thinking they were straight-forward *per capita* figures—and not based on a shaky formula? The report went on to look at the variation in the number of full-time-equivalent GPs:

> There are overall *fewer GPs per head* of weighted population in the East and North of London (*where health need is greatest*), compared with the South and West.[25]

In this quotation, the italicised phrases can only reinforce the already established deception of the unwary reader. In company with Goodier, Darzi cannot evade the charge of either unconscious or deliberate deception. Two conditions are necessary for this particular deception to be called 'unconscious'. Firstly, Darzi and his team must have thought the formula so obviously fair that they did not need to mention that there is widespread dispute about it. Secondly, they must have been unaware that the general reader would be easily misled by the wording around a technicality—and that they therefore had an obligation to be careful not to abuse the power of simple phrases. We need a word twixt 'unconscious' and 'deliberate' for such deception—by individuals in powerful positions, whose belief that the formula is fair is so strong that they do not need to reveal their private faith. Would 'spinning' suffice for that?

More acceptable than deception, delusion can come from honest incompetence in statistical modelling—but it can have malign consequences, as it did in Annex F of the DoH chief economic adviser's response[26] to the Health Committee. The modelling was a fine example of the sort already deployed by the Glasgow team and that motivated Ed Leamer's *cri de coeur:*

> Let's take the con out of econometrics![27]

Annex F tabulated the results of the many-variable least-squares fitting of ten models. None of the variables had any relationship to the concept of *managerial ability* (taken to be unobservable)—but the outputs of the preferred model were nevertheless used to put 'weak management' in the firing line as one of the causes of large deficits (perhaps the major one):

> Organisations with large deficits are frequently found to have had weak management capacity... weak management may exacerbate the underlying causes and result in large deficits. ... The model reported here systematically under-predicts extreme in-year balances (large surplus or large deficit) and this suggests that we are missing a key driver (or drivers) of deficits *such as managerial ability*.[28]

The model was supposed to explain the 'in-year balance' for 2004/5 of the 303 'health economies' (PCTs with the trusts they serve). From its output, a remarkable graph plotted 'forecast error' or 'residual' as the y-axis against *the same in-year balance* as the x-axis. (A residual is defined as the in-year balance minus its fitted value. *En masse,* residuals are usually regarded as uninformative once the model that generated them has been accepted.) My italics are to reassure statisticians that this was what was actually done—that the residuals were indeed plotted against the dependent variable (in-year balance). This is what Annex F had to say about the graph:

> The model forecast errors (*residuals*) show the extent to which the model under-predicts (+) or over-predicts (−) the in-year balance. We observe a strong positive correlation between the variables. *Such an observation is consistent with our hypothesis that we are missing the unobservable managerial ability variable from the model.*[29]

The remarkable graph is pure artefact. Its wayward logic can be illustrated with materials from the popular press. In place of 'health economies' think of 303 randomly selected Englishmen. Instead of 'in-year balance' as the variable to be 'forecast', use body mass index (BMI). Instead of a 'battery of explanatory variables', use a single variable—the sign of the zodiac (month of birth). A 'formula' that will forecast BMI is then no more than a set of 12 numbers—one for each zodiacal sign. The formula fitted by the Annex F method would be the monthly averages of BMI in the sample of 303 men. Those of us who are not yet under zodiacal influence can be expected to agree that those averages could all be the same number—as near as makes no difference. The residuals would then be obtained by subtracting this common value from the 303 BMI values, and the scatterplot of residual against BMI would be even more spuriously convincing than the graph that encouraged the chief economic adviser to malign management. The DoH logic would allow speculation about zodiacal responsibility for the obese state of the nation.

In other words, make sure you are using a poor forecasting model and the sky is limit—no conjecture is beyond confirmation. By the usual criteria, DoH's model for the remarkable graph is a poor one—it 'explains' only 34 per cent of the variation of in-year balance, leaving 66 per cent for idle speculation.

Direct measurement

While it can be safely concluded that the current formula has no rational basis, the question of whether or not it is deviating in the right direction[30] from national equality can be decisively resolved only by the largely unexplored alternative of direct measurement of healthcare need—which would have to get down to the level of individual patients. The practicality of direct measurement depends on whether one could collect the necessary morbidity data and find enough consensus on difficult priorities to arrive at a socially-agreed and financially-supportable measure of real need. An impromptu and clearly refinable suggestion of how direct measurement might be introduced emerged in my oral evidence to the Health Committee:

> Health cost is a variable thing. It is applied to IVF and it is applied to cancer. You cannot aggregate all of this together but you have got to use value judgement. That is why direct measurement has to address the serious problems [and] go to a sampling of GP-registered patients in a pilot study ... I would use a small fraction of the money that I believe has been wasted by this formula (a very small fraction) to investigate, using trained nurses, sampling patients—some of whom will not have had any costs on the Health Service in the previous year. So, fine—that is a zero and then forget about it, but other patients will have had certain calls on the Health Service. A trained nurse would be able [to estimate], as near as one could ... , the real health need of [a] patient. And then there would be another committee ... to put pounds on this and say what this really costs. But that would bring up the question of value judgements.[31]

Contact with individuals in a project to measure healthcare need from a large stratified random sample of GP-patients would sideline the econometric assumptions and pretensions that undermine the present approach.

Even before the Milburn formula had done a year's work, an independent group of researchers supported by the

Economic & Social Research Council were finding evidence that gave focus to their doubts about an approach that relied so heavily on econometric theory. They used Health Survey of England data to get closer to the alternative of direct measurement. Their study[32] suggested that there may be a marked bias in the relative weighting that the formula gives to the variations between PCTs of the indices for age-profile and additional-needs—a bias that could be wrongly favouring PCTs with a youngish age-profile and expectation of life well below average but not yet needing much health care—over PCTs with an aged age-profile where the expectation of life is well above average but there is a need for health care when that expectation meets the buffers. That was the conclusion reported by Sheena Asthana and Alex Gibson (professor of health policy and research fellow at Plymouth University, respectively) in their written evidence to the Health Committee.[33]

The Committee can be excused for not getting to grips with the exceedingly complex provenance and structure of the formula itself. It was judicially reserved[34] about the concerns that many witnesses had expressed about the elusive concept of fairness:

> We do not consider ourselves qualified to judge whether these concerns are justified.[35]

But there was a crumb of comfort for those witnesses—and for those who favoured direct measurement:

> We recommend that the formula be reviewed. Consideration should be given to basing the formula on actual need rather than proxies of need.[36]

Some changes are in the air! ACRA and DoH have commissioned three separate research groups. One group was asked to refine the current formula. Its report[37] has been responsible for a change in the formula for the years 2009 to

2011. However, there is no evidence that the more flexible statistical modelling for the change that has been made to just one part of the formula takes us any closer to truth and reality about the geographical variation of healthcare need. The two other research groups are competing in the design of more significant changes to make the resource allocation more 'person-based'—that was the keyword in the invitation to tender to which the groups responded. It is to be hoped that at least one of these two will get closer to the goal of direct measurement.

2

Water Under the Bridge or Lessons to be Learned?

The PCT-funding issue is still very much alive. January 2009 saw publication of a defence of the formula in a report that has been 'revised to read as a retrospective review of June 2008'.[1] It was commissioned by the Secretary of State in 2006, in the year she was questioned about the formula by the Health Committee. The report's author is an LSE professor of management science who made little attempt to defend the formula on technical grounds but employed the usual arts[2] to persuade his readers that there is 'much to be proud of in the development of capitation formulas for the NHS in England',[3] before breaking new ground by recommending that DoH publish 'the rationale of the current formula and accounts of alternatives that ACRA has explored and why these have been rejected'.[4]

Here are four now-fading projects that still have much to teach us—and one that has not yet had the exposure that its remarkable and financially damaging formula should command.

Water privatisation

In 1989, UCL's department of statistical science was approached by a firm of civil engineers contracted by the government to look after the public interest in the forthcoming water privatisation. The job was to scrutinise the statistical cases that ten water authorities had submitted for the high charges that would be needed to meet new quality standards for the industry. The main problem (still with us) was with the mileages of clogged or leaking underground pipes that would cost many millions of pounds to replace. These mileages had somehow to be estimated from small amounts of costly data already in hand. The estimates were to be translated into replacement costs to help the privatisation regulator determine the 'K-factors' that would control customers' water bills.

The statistical methods varied greatly between authorities. Some analyses had been done by legal firms claiming to have the necessary expertise. Some of the authorities used so-called 'classical' estimates based entirely on observations on the condition of randomly unearthed pipes, using standard statistical methods in widespread use. But, in two cases, the statistical methods were innovatingly 'neo-Bayesian' in spirit—allowing an interested party to adjust the measurements with prior knowledge based on an in-house expertise that could be approved by the scrutinising engineers.[5] My highly critical review of all the statistical work went to the regulator—under a veil of commercial secrecy. For all I know, subsequent decisions may have avoided any betrayal of the public interest by an excessive generosity in the K-factors from poor statistical work.

Few clues about the contractual machinery of departmental soft science can be gleaned from this commercially confidential case. It is for others to consider how commercial sensitivity in such public services may adversely affect the integrity of decision making. But questions could still be asked, by those authorised to do so, that might resolve residual doubts about the contested K-factors for water charges and the statistical procedures for their periodic re-estimation. There must be some doubts because, at the time of writing, two of the privatised companies—Southern Water and Severn Trent—have been fined by the OfWat regulator for statistical deceptions (£20 million and £36 million respectively). At the same time, Ofwat has reduced by £3 million a fine of £12.5 million on Thames Water for providing inadequate regulatory information—because, so it was said, the firm's processes were so bad it did not know it had breached the rule![6]

Getting the measure of the police

Geoffrey Robinson joined the Treasury as paymaster general in 1997. Representing the wisdom of the private sector, he assembled the Public Services Productivity Panel to bring that wisdom into a government determined 'to see a step change in national productivity'. Clare Spottiswoode, a senior partner in PA Consulting Ltd, produced the fifth report of the panel—on police productivity.[7] The technical work was done by a combined Treasury/Home Office team. The outside contracts went to economists whose recommendations gave a 'state of the art' halo to an econometric technique dating from 1957 but now known as data envelopment analysis (DEA) following its rediscovery in 1978. DEA technique and its bells and whistles are now taught as received wisdom in leading universities. It has become the purportedly scientific basis of a huge consultancy industry. Critical analyses of its pretensions are thin on the ground compared with the huge literature that supports it.[8]

It was for 'identifying' the historical technique as a 'new way' to measure police force efficiency that the chief secretary to the Treasury expressed gratitude to Clare Spottiswoode—which was, somewhat ungraciously, belied by her saying that DEA offered only a 'second-best' approach, since the 'underlying monopoly' problem was being managed but not solved.[9] Within two years, Home Office and Treasury were persuaded by uncontracted outside opinion and internal democracy to see DEA as a technical cul de sac. PricewaterhouseCoopers[10] was brought in to pronounce the last rites—a ceremony from which the Royal Statistical Society was excluded.[11] The productivities of the 43 police forces of England were then assessed by so-called spidergrams—to the dismay of those economists who still support DEA as 'state of the art'.

The unacceptable features of DEA were only slowly recognised because its distinctive feature was initially seen as a strength—DEA would allow each police force to make its own allocation of resources, delivering different outcomes in response to local priorities, and still manage to get a high efficiency grading. The simple idea was that it would be reasonable to award 100 per cent to any police force with the lowest cost among all the other police forces *with the same output profile*. Otherwise, the force would be said to be to some degree *technically inefficient*. This would give all forces an incentive to perform well while maintaining local priorities. That sounds good until you read it twice. To satisfy the public, the Home Office has to specify a wide range of different kinds of output from which local priorities can be chosen—but with only 43 police forces there can be no other comparison forces with even roughly the same output profile with respect to every output.

To conceal the problem, DEA salesmen rely on *virtuals*—in this case, an infinity of diaphanous police forces created only by abstract econometric conceptualisations. In that infinity, there *will* be a sub-infinity with precisely the same output levels as any real-world police force put up for efficiency grading—its 'efficiency' is then a question of how close the force gets to the lowest cost in that sub-infinity. That is where Catch 22 comes into play! With only 43 forces, the geometry and arithmetic means that, if you specify enough outputs to meet what people want from the police, DEA would award a generously high efficiency grading to almost every force—especially any force that abuses the 'local priority' dispensation by, for example, concentrating on its response time to 999 calls.

The generosity would have been a problem for the Home Office if it had ever had to think about what to make of a column of 'efficiencies' so devised. The problem for the public was in DEA's diversion of attention from the necessary and unavoidably subjective valuation of different sorts of output. DEA is an attractive technique for anyone who prefers permissiveness to 'value-judgementalism'. The Spottiswoode report rejected advice that they should consider the simpler (less 'state of the art') approach in which outputs are weighted by *nationally agreed societal weights* to give an overall performance measure. One of the experts whose advice had been rejected, Professor Chris Watkins, put the argument against DEA in a nutshell at an *ad hoc* meeting of the Royal Statistical Society's (RSS) Official Statistics Section:[12]

> The property of DEA that allows multiple outputs to be assessed in the most favourable light for each unit being assessed is perhaps excusable in awarding classes of university degree, but not in the training of surgeons or in the activities of police forces. This property could be described as a *post-hoc* definition of allocative efficiency.

By 2002, there were over 3,000 publications about DEA by over 2,000 authors since its rediscovery in 1978. It must have been difficult for civil servants not to be impressed by such a large industry. In 2003, the Department for Education and Skills awarded a contract for research on the cost structure of the higher education sector in England. The invitation to tender—which invoked the government's commitment to 'increasing the participation rate among 18-30 year-olds ... towards 50 per cent by 2010'—had sensibly suggested a wide range of avenues that needed to be explored. But the contract went to a team of university economists and operational researchers who confidently pressed their specialised expertise in DEA as a technique for ranking universities! Then again, in 2004, DoH civil servants seeking advice about DEA told me that they had in mind some application of DEA to the NHS. What kind of production units were they thinking of? Will the National Archive tell us one day what happened to these two departmental forays into the unknown?

The police productivity study appears to have been under firm political control from the start—with reliance on a Treasury-appointed committee of business and public sector leaders. The Treasury appears to have left the hiring of consultants to Home Office economists. Statutory contractual arrangements allowed the range of approaches to the problem to be narrowed down to 'state of the art' proposals. These were then allowed, for a while, to over-rule expressions of doubt about DEA by some Home Office civil servants and in Treasury documents of earlier years. The possibility of a more open-ended approach had been rejected but, in the end, that came from a conjunction of an accidental incursion of outside opinion triggering a surge of departmental heterarchy.

'Speed Cameras—the truth'

How, thus, did the embarrassing concept of 'truth' get on the cover of a Royal Statistical Society journal in connection with speed cameras?[13] The answer dates from 1996 when the Transport Research Laboratory (TRL) was privatised and a PriceWaterhouse cost-benefit study[14] claimed that cameras paid for themselves five times in the first year of operation alone, once the full benefits to society are considered. The claim was eventually recognised as statistically worthless because it took no account of 'selection bias' (see below). In 1998, the Treasury under a new chancellor allowed police forces to use fines from cameras to pay for more cameras. The safety camera partnership programme started in 2000 with a pilot study in eight police force areas. With TRL privatised, the Department of Transport (DoT) was free to give the contract for managing the programme to PA Consulting Ltd, whose first report to DoT expressed no doubt about the underlying science—the project had become a 'partnership' overseen by representatives of 11 'stakeholders'.

Lack of scientific direction led to what has clearly been a lost opportunity to obtain hard experimental evidence about different ways of deploying cameras to reduce excessive speed and the associated casualties. By the time PA Consulting came to write its second report, questions were being raised about what the project data were revealing on these issues of public concern, and whether what was revealed would justify expansion of the programme in the particular form that had been adopted—one-eyed yellow boxes on fixed poles. For example, the project appears to have ignored the question of any relationship between the selection of sites for camera installation and the informativeness of the data about speeds and accidents associated with those installations. There seems to have been little thinking about how to make those data more informative e.g by experimental design that might have incorporated the 'gold standard' of experimentally randomised control.

PA Consulting turned to UCL's Centre for Transport Studies for the statistical modelling on which purely observational (non-experimental) studies have to rely. In 2004, their joint report was made available to the BBC for a *Today* programme 'tribunal' of arguments for and against speed cameras and road humps.[15] The then Secretary of State for Transport, Alastair Darling, was badly advised to claim that the report had established that the cameras were reducing accidents by 40 per cent and saving over 100 lives a year. In fact, the report had been unable to deal at all satisfactorily with a statistical artefact of which the UCL researchers were only too well aware—what Francis Galton had called 'regression to the mean' and is more easily understood as a form of *selection bias*. The selection of camera installation sites raises ethical considerations. It is largely dictated by the recent occurrence of serious or fatal accidents on the associated stretch of road. This will inevitably bias the selection of sites towards those that have experienced a fortuitously high number of accidents, which then returns to a lower level after the installation. Some fraction of the aggregate observed reduction will therefore be artefactual.

Uncertainty about statistics was red meat for that section of the British public that had by 2004 developed an almost irrational animus against speed cameras. The Official Statistics Section of the Royal Statistical Society tried to boost the science when it organised a meeting at which Dr Linda Mountain of Liverpool University suggested how the selection bias might be estimated. The audience included DfT civil servants and DfT's chief scientific adviser. Meanwhile, the PA/UCL collaboration extended their analyses to cover another year's data from the participating safety camera partners with, by then, about 4,000 cameras. Their report did not appear by the expected date and DfT announced that no new speed cameras would be installed for several months, as the government awaited the report. A spokeswoman said it was important to get things right.

When it appeared six months later, the report[16] had a technical appendix by Linda Mountain and colleague, suggesting that casualty savings may have been over-estimated by a factor of three. That matters when any attempt is made to put the benefit of reductions against the high cost of the safety camera programme. It may still be the case that benefit outweighs cost even when the necessary downward adjustment of savings are made, but there is a much wider cost-benefit framework than the one that considers only the performance of safety cameras at fixed sites. It is one that would assess the benefits of very different road safety measures using speed cameras, from so-called 'average speed' systems to detection of dangerous driving by mobile 'traffic cops'.

At the start, Treasury control of the safety camera partnership programme was total, when it was also called a 'cost recovery system'. Lateral thinking was side-lined by fiat rather than as a consequence of the contractual machinery process. The reasons for ultimate failure are now well understood. In his statement to Parliament, Mr Darling recognised that it was 'timely that camera activity and partnerships are integrated into the wider road safety delivery process'. Britain has the expertise to do that, provided its enrolment can be given the necessary scientific independence.

Figures of fancy

Well before eight East European countries joined the EU in 2004, policy-making civil servants in the Home Office's Immigration and Nationality Directorate (IND) must have been anticipating ministerial requests for arguments for or against imposing post-accession restrictions on immigration for work. They commissioned econometricians led by UCL's Christian Dustmann to predict the post-accession migration flows to the UK. Their 'projection' was canonised as the now notorious confidence interval of 'between 5,000 and 13,000 net immigrants per year'.[17]

Appearing before the Commons Select Committee on Home Affairs & European Security in 2006, minister Liam Byrne was asked whether he thought the discrepancy between predictions and the numbers that came would have justified imposing the restrictions that EU would allow. Mr Byrne thought the evidence showed no negative impacts on employment and would not have made the case for restrictions. Mr Byrne's aside—that 'despite the cheque it got from the Home Office' the econometric team 'did not get the projections quite right'—suggests that the government believes it has to buy, and can expect to buy, truth from universities.[18]

Nearly a year later, the House of Lords Economic Affairs Committee challenged Professor Dustmann to account for the discrepancy between the 5,000-13,000 figures and 'the much larger number' who have come.[19] He was able to explain that his figures were for the net annual flow over the first ten years in which return migration would be quite large, that one could not expect 'robust' predictions when there was such a dearth of relevant historical information, and that, in any case, his report was based on the assumption that the large European economies, such as Germany and Italy, would open their borders to East European migrants as well. That assumption puzzled chairman Lord Wakeham who thought that it was wrong—that Germany had made clear its intention to have the maximum seven-year transition period. But, once the 'wrong' assumption was made, the model for the 5,000-13,000 predictions could be (and was) based on analogous modelling *before 2001* by two German econometricians. So the IND contract had been formally fulfilled by a model that was neither designed nor able to allow for any effect of transitional restriction by Germany! The assumption was also known to be wrong for an appreciable time during which the Home Office trumpeted the reassuring 5,000-13,000 figures. The reassurance was repeated until the reality of the increasing numbers put a stop to it.

The Dustmann report cannot be criticised for not warning the Home Office about the number of weaknesses in its forecasts. Its executive summary listed four caveats, any one of which could have inhibited immigration minister Beverley Hughes from telling MPs that the number coming here for employment will be minimal. In effect, the caveats were:

a. There was hardly any historical migration to the UK from the eight East European countries i.e. nothing to go on.

b. The gap was filled by collecting migration data for 35 countries or areas around the world (none in Europe) for the 26 years 1975-2000, and by assuming that a statistically sophisticated model fitted to those data could be used to make predictions for Europe for the ten years from 2004 to 2014.

c. Even those data were based on the UK's International Passenger Survey—an unreliable and parsimonious sampling of those coming in and out of the major ports of entry.

d. Migrations from the 35 countries or areas were subject to a variety of regulations and particular programmes, which were not taken into account when doing the estimations.

The Dustmann report ended the list with English understatement—that the predictions had to be evaluated with some caution. My UCL research paper[20] on the report expressed puzzlement about whether it was a technical exercise, honest study or convenient obfuscation—or, as I concluded, something of all three. The arbitrary choice of model was reminiscent of the statistical witchcraft for the PCT-funding formula and the dearth of scepticism about it suggested an academic exercise in technique. The explicit caveats already noted were suggestive of an honest study. As for convenient obfuscation, that is a charge for the Home Office to refute, not the authors of the report. There is, however, a broader question for UCL that cannot be brushed aside. The study reveals the willingness of a renowned university department to oblige a government clearly looking for politically exploitable research—that it would then describe as 'independent'. In what way would departmental teaching and research be enriched by such a foreseeably futile academic exercise?

For this book, the key question is about the contractual machinery. The research that ended with the 5,000-13,000 prediction must have been overseen by intelligent civil servants in the Home Office. Did no-one question the seriousness of the research proposal that got the contract? How many 'expressions of interest' had there been? How many competing tenders were submitted—and how serious could they have been if they were judged inferior to the successful tender?

My final case exhibits not water under the bridge but a still surrounding inundation pouring through a topsy-turvey formula of Lewis Carroll quality.

Local government lunacy

The Department of Communities and Local Government (DCLG) uses a formula to distribute well over £20 billion of central government taxes to 456 local 'authorities' in England—councils, police authorities and fire services. This so-called *Revenue Support Grant* is to complement the direct expenditure of council-tax money. The formula (the so-called 'four-block method') has an arithmetic complexity whose logic has defied understanding—even by those who devised it. Its consequences have been noticed, though, especially by rural authorities (for 2008-09, shires are getting less than half as much per head of their population as London does). Two academics were asked to investigate the inequity but were (serendipitally) diverted by a remarkable discovery. This was when they made an engagingly simple test of the robustness of the formula—*by leaving an authority out of the calculation, putting the money it now gets back into the kitty and rerunning the calculation as if the authority had never existed!* Think of a mother of an extended family that has tea together every Sunday. Routinely, as if to a formula, she cuts the cake into the same unequal portions, one for each family member—with an extremely thin slice for grandmother. One Sunday, granny is sick and cannot join in. Would that make any substantial difference to the slices the others get?

When the researchers left out Bolton—one of the large authorities—the proportions of the now somewhat larger cake for the remaining 455 authorities changed only slightly. However, when puny Wokingham—the authority getting the smallest grant of under £8 million—was left out, the consequences were surrealistic. For example, Thames Valley Police lost £14 million while Birmingham gained £38 million! That means that a number of authorities would be asked to accept appreciably lower funding so that some authorities, such as Birmingham, would profit from an overall increase in the size of the cake. Come in, Ombudsman!

This is the 'unbelievable truth' that must now be acknowledged. The formula is so lacking in robustness that, without exaggeration, one can say that its tail of poorly-funded authorities is wagging the whole of the dog. Add less than £8 million to what the Treasury distributes to 455 authorities and the formula goes haywire—spewing out massive changes in the slices they get. All because the least-favoured authority is excluded from the calculation and not allowed to influence what it does, except by a small act of generosity! One must hope that, once DCLG has verified the research findings—for which no contracted expertise should be necessary—they do not shoot the messengers. How *will* such an outrageous finding be greeted by DCLG and its host of 'independent' advisers?

3

Breaking the National Silence

Ignorance, indifference and knowingness

At the heart of the cacophony of political discourse in England today, there is an eerie silence about the quality and expense of the policy-making research contracted out by government departments. What we have instead is a melée of political discussion and backchat that skims the surface but fails to get to the heart of things when it matters. The public, including the opinion-forming class, is fed reassuring and infantilising morsels daily, of which the anaesthetic potential may largely explain the silence. Mental laziness may be doing the rest. Unless one is contracted to do so, thinking about technical detail can be an unrewarding and exhausting activity when there are so many other more exciting activities to engage in. There is great reluctance, by those capable of doing so, to monitor what is going on in the policy-making world.

Consider the silence that has enveloped the manifestly contestable issues of the structure and provenance of England's PCT-funding formula. It is a test-bed for what ought to be general concern about the state of intellectual exchange in third millenium Britain. There are three sorts of silence about the formula. To start with, there is the one sanctioned by *ignorance* maintained willy-nilly by the (silent) majority of the population of England—most of us cannot even identify our own PCT! So it is hardly surprising that we are unaware that the NHS gets for each of us an amount of money that varies by a large factor from PCT to PCT—at the behest of a six-year-old formula from the North. Equally understandable is the variety of silence based on *indifference*

—an influential swathe of the population believes it has satisfactory private health cover, either in England or in some overseas haven. Widespread ignorance and indifference helps to explain why those who wish to expose and reform the current resource allocation formula have made little progress. But it is the silence that can be said to be *knowing* that may be exercising a larger and more influential negative influence.

There are three public platforms, outside the realms of government, that are well placed to defy any silence acting against the public interest—the universities, the BBC with its flagship Radio 4 channel and the Royal Statistical Society.

Universities

One would have to consult several decades of DoH archives to get the history of the involvement of universities in the design of resource allocation formulae for the NHS—an involvement that takes the form of a succession of contractual engagements of university research teams. Each team accepts a remit from DoH and reveals its thinking as a *post hoc* rationalisation of the formula ultimately delivered. There may have been fierce arguments (methodological, political and principled) within each team while it was doing its work—as well as within the DoH-appointed and carefully guarded groups of overseers (RAG, TAG, ACRA). If so, little of these arguments has emerged in any forum that could engage the attention of more than one university discipline.

A relevant factor in England has been the proliferation of departments of 'health economics'—a disciplinary label that might have been wish fulfilment to DoH mandarins. When the opportunity became available to widen the debate or to inform those who are pleading for enlightenment, what we got was a contribution to the country's deafening silence about the formula—and, enveloped in it, the academic caravan moved on. What excuses can be offered for this arguably unhealthy state of affairs? Does Benveniste's moral reproach from 1970s' California match the reality here?:

> Those experts who ... believe they are responsible only for a narrow spectrum of technical knowledge and who fail to assume their political responsibility become agents of bureaucratic sterility.[1]

If anything, the reality here is that research teams producing funding formulae range over an academic spectrum too wide for their dominant expertise and are only too willing to take on a political role.

For policy-making in general, changes in universities over recent decades have handed moral responsibility to line managers. The transfer matters little for the bulk of university research—from traditional individual scholarship to expensive scientific research funded by research councils or industry. It does matter for the soft scientific research that is directly funded by government departments using statutory contractual machinery. It matters because that kind of research encroaches on matters of moral and ethical sensitivity. Heads of university departments are under constant pressure to win contracts and individual researchers list the grants they have attracted on their personal web-pages. Such financial pressures can only inhibit the between-university or between-department within-university controversies that should still be the hallmark of an academic life and the essential feedstuff of its proper purpose. To stay in business, universities have to compete for lucrative government contracts. At the end of a university seminar on the Spottiswoode Report, a lecturer expressed horror at the part played in it by some universities and suggested I approach a journalist about it. I stopped nodding my half-agreement when a wiser head told me that 'things' were 'different now'. Too many of us have to serve the financial interests of our institution or department, sometimes by an unhealthily close relationship with government departments, and then remain knowingly silent on the contestable isues that we could help to resolve.

The British Broadcasting Corporation

Many of the daily battles that government fights with the media are on just one small battle-ground—the BBC's *Today* programme on Radio 4. Few would imagine that silence plays any role in the minds of the editors of that programme—but I believe there is forensic evidence of just that.

My Exhibit A is that the *Today* editors have chosen to remain silent on the issue that so concerned the Health Committee, namely the 'fairness' of the PCT-funding formula. For that issue, there is contentious material that could have been presented in a way that would have engaged the attention of the *Today* audience for the few minutes that such items require. It would be unreasonable to expect the BBC to adjudicate the issue—as it had done, tongue-in-cheek, for speed cameras. But a revelation by *Today* would not have passed unnoticed—that a formula that might be causing damaging PCT deficits had been produced by statistical methods spurned by statisticians. One month after the Health Committee report on NHS Deficits, there was a week-long series of *Today* pieces about the problems of the NHS. An interview with Patricia Hewitt was followed by Ed Stourton congratulating the public on its successful 'civilian journalism' because it had 'attracted the attention of Tony Blair'. Blair was interviewed the next day by John Humphrys after listeners had been guided live 'through the thickets of NHS statistics' by the reporter's 'statistical expert'—health economist Professor John Appleby of the King's Fund. My disappointment with the whole week's broadcasts was expressed in a letter to the *Daily Telegraph*, telling readers that an opportunity had been missed to broadcast the question that chairman Kevin Barron had put at the start of his committee's inquiry: 'Is the funding formula used to allocate resources to PCTs fair?'.

Exhibit B materialised when economist and leading presenter Evan Davis moved to the spaciousness of a blog[2] to 'figure out' for his audience what net immigration at current levels means for housing. Picking up a report suggesting that an extra 200 homes a day would have to be built for at least the next two decades, Davis notes that:

> If we build at that rate for two decades, at the current density of 40 homes per hectare, the area covered would be 19 by 19 kilometres.

The 'evanomic' arithmetic is that 200 x (20 x 365 + 5 for leap years)/40 = 36,525 hectares which is 19.1 x 19.1 kms. He does not say 'only 19' but seeds the idea with a 'worth looking at' graphic of a small square hovering over England somewhere between Sheffield and Nottingham. When placed over a good road map of Birmingham, it only just covers that city as we know it—and its population of about a million. The blog does not refer to the Government Actuary's projection of a population increase of five millions from which the 200 homes figure was derived. It purports to be a balanced analysis of the pros and cons of continued immigration at the current level, with an appeal to complexity:

> the reason why we can simultaneously hold optimistic or pessimistic views is that its effects are often quite complicated.

But a more balanced presentation might have mentioned population numbers and dealt with the corollary to the arithmetic—that optimism based on the implied 'only 19' relies on being able to shrink the area of the vibrant city of Birmingham by a factor of five without shrinking its population. That there may be more than art, in all of that, is suggested by the same presenter's exultant aside to an interviewee[3] in July 2008 that the last ten years had seen an increasing influence of economics on Number 10—in recognition, presumably, of that discipline's evidence-based policy-making and stress on data in a variety of areas.

Today's James Naughtie provided a simple but revealing Exhibit C when one morning in 2008 he solicitously announced that most people were surprised by the large number of immigrants from Eastern European countries after their accession to the European Union in 2004. That may be because *Today's* editors had down-played their reporting of the controversy about the statistical predictions—a controversy that had been public knowledge from other sources for months before accession.

Bias by silent knowingness or reporting deficit appears to be part of *Today's* make-up. On many issues, the BBC appears to see itself as proprietor rather than custodian of the public interest—a vision that is most clearly manifested in the confidence of the *Today* programme presenters that they are able to wrap up complex issues in the simple packages that their commuting or breakfasting listeners are thought to appreciate. Even the third of the BBC's Reithian missions—'to inform, educate and *entertain'*—would justify more broadcasting time for serious analysis of policy-making controversies than we get from present programme scheduling. There are other sections of the media—tabloids with screaming headlines and satirists such as Rory Bremner on Channel 4—whose influence on government policy-making may, from time to time, exceed that of the BBC. However, none of these can be called to account as legitimately as can a body fed by over three billions a year of legally enforced taxation.

The Royal Statistical Society

The Royal Statistical Society (RSS) may be the only platform from which reform of the government's soft science can be effectively propagated. RSS has over 7,000 members, many of whom are civil servants employed in the Government Statistical Service (GSS). The collection and classification of data for government became what is now the daily task of the Office of National Statistics (ONS). Those data are our 'national statistics'. Ministers in departments of state are free to define what it is that makes a particular statistic National. Over time, a polite stand-off has emerged between RSS and government, associated with a division between National Statistics and their logical complement—official government statistics that are not national but that may be called departmental statistics. RSS has no recognised standing in relation to routine departmental statistical activity or its role in the policy-making that largely determines the welfare of the nation.

In his retirement address,[4] RSS president Tim Holt spoke with five years' experience as director of ONS and head of GSS. During his presidency, RSS has been formulating and strongly representing to government its consensual views about the shape of the Statistics and Registration Services Act of 2007 and the new Board of Statistics. The following string of quotations from the president's address is therefore both well-informed and authoritative:

> A key question for the Society is how statistics and statistical thinking might have an even greater influence on public policy and decision making than it now does... [The Act of 2007 is] still not of a form and content that the Society would have chosen... [To build public confidence, the new act depends on] an environment within government which creates space to demonstrate professional independence and statistical integrity.... [The] Board must not limit its strategic oversight to the Office of National Statistics alone but must span the entire system... It should promote practices and policies that take account of the public interest... statisticians may be viewed [by policy officials] as unhelpful to the policy promotion function and hence may be excluded from the policy development function. Statistical producers in policy departments may sometimes be unwilling to press the professional independence

> issue too far for fear of this outcome... The Society is concerned to ensure that statistics are used fully and effectively wherever they are needed throughout the public sector. Consequently, it would be a mistake to imagine that, if we wish to promote the use of statistics and statistical thinking for evidence-based policy, we should seek to influence only or even primarily the GSS... Much of the public output of the GSS falls into [the] category of what one might term the 'statistical wallpaper'... There are many areas where statistical analysis is or should be a cornerstone of the government's policy development and there is no link to the GSS... The Society is as concerned to ensure that statistics are used effectively in these areas as in the regular outputs of the GSS... There are numerous examples of Ministers or government departments establishing advisory panels on issues for which there is a core statistical element. Almost always these panels have no recognised statistical expert as a member. Recognition within government of when statistical expertise could usefully contribute is woeful... there are plenty of examples where policies are adopted on what appears to be flimsy empirical evidence.

This book has already provided additional evidence of the significant truth of Tim Holt's observations. Do they go far enough? RSS has paid little attention to the contractual machinery with which departmental policy-making is serviced. Papers in the Society's journals have revealed that, even when policies have an essentially statistical core, the technical expertise has been contracted to those in other disciplines for whom statistical methods are but imported items in their toolkit. Even if RSS has maintained corporate silence about that particularly sensitive issue, it is a 'knowing' silence that might one day speak volumes.

4

Breaching Whitehall Confidentiality

The ungrasped nettle in the policy-making garden is that ministers, with responsibilty for policy, can claim they must have confidentiality for the necessary professional advice—and then validate policy by maintaining that the invoked advice was independent. In our most documentable scandal (the PCT funding formula) confidentiality was, and continues to be, maintained about the proceedings of ACRA and its Technical Advisory Group (TAG). A reporter for the *Health Service Journal* enquiring into the stop-gap resource allocations for 2008-09 was reminded by DoH that the work of ACRA was 'confidential and restricted'.[1]

Those questioning the formula get the soft words that turn away wrath. DoH's chief economic adviser told the Health Committee that DoH believes in taking advice from recognised authorities and has set up:

> an independent panel [ACRA] that comprises senior clinicians, economists and statisticians to advise it.[2]

That body was more accurately described as an 'independent body made up of NHS managers, academics and GPs' by Lord Warner in answer to a parliamentary question from Lord Campbell-Savours.[3] When the Health Committee began its inquiry, ACRA was made up of six DoH employees, five NHS chief executives, five people with GP affiliations, a research council chief executive and two academics—a health economist and a 'social exclusionist'. Did these busy people have time for more than superficial analysis of the funding formula? Were they even qualified to do that? There is no-one on the advisory committee from the Treasury to influence or simply observe the thinking about how a fifth of public expenditure is to be carved up by formula. The list refutes the oft-repeated description of the committee as 'independent'—however convincingly its few members from outside DoH or NHS can show that they are. DoH's finance director was only rejecting his own Aunt Sally when he told the Health Committee he could not 'envisage a situation where the Government would actually put the distribution of resources across the whole NHS into an entirely independent body'.[4]

Diana Woodhouse[5] had a message for confidentiality addicts in a wide-ranging analysis of the sad state of public administration concerning case-law. She quoted a judge in the 1992 'Oral Snuff' case who:

> did not accept the submission made on behalf of the Secretary of State that it was not in accordance with good administration to reveal technical advice given to Ministers by scientific experts because to do so might inhibit the giving of candid advice. He commented, 'For my part I regard the submission as having no realistic basis at all ... I cannot believe that scientists of the quality to be expected to be serving on a committee of this kind would be in any way inhibited if their conclusions were revealed to interested parties.'

What is ACRA[6] for? Since its creation in the Nineties, what has it done other than rubber-stamp a resource allocation formula that has no rational basis? One can quite understand why ministers, or any senior civil servant for that matter, should want to have private and confidential consultations with independent experts at the stage when policies have not yet been determined—when minds are still open to a broad range of half-baked possibilities. It is quite another matter when such confidentiality is invoked to defend already decided or implemented policies—especially those that involve huge public expenditure—by claiming that those policies are validated by the 'authority' that those 'independent' experts represent. Once decided, policies and the processes behind them should be open to scrutiny of the reasoning for which 'independent authority' is claimed. Putting such a principle into practice would require big changes to the relevant contractual machinery of government and would therefore be a matter for Parliament to address.

Sir Christopher Foster's *cri de coeur* about the state we are in proposes fourteen 'pillars' of support for an improved machinery of government. None of them relate to the dark corner of the machinery room that protects ministerial claims to confidentiality for the advice the minister gets from advisory committees or special advisers. Foster's fourteenth pillar, Objectivity and Openness, comes close to a demand that there be more light in that departmental corner. It does so by requiring that:

> when an argument is made, it should be logical, and that the relevant evidence should be presented with an assessment of its relevance. What different audiences—other ministers, Parliament, those directly affected, and the general public—need [in order] to make an honest and well-based assessment for their own purposes will and should vary.[7]

How could such democratic enlightenment have been achieved in the policy-making of the PCT-funding formula? All the evidence suggests that it is the contractual machinery that, step by step, pushed the department into a corner—where it now has to stay, well and truly painted, until the paint is eroded by the passage of time and DoH can step out into new territory. There is a damaging inflexibility in the ordained procedure that is amazing to outside observers who have been privileged to get a sense of what goes on. Such observers should move beyond their amazement and suggest possible ways of doing things better. Parliamentarians and former civil servants may then be able to give the suggestions a legal shape—a fifteenth Fosterian pillar, as it were, to stand alongside the fourteenth as its statutory enforcer.

5

A Lost Battle of Lords?

Haldanian principle

For Foster, 'tradition' embodied a principle that had grown out of the Northcote/Trevelyan reform of the nineteenth century. The 'Carltona principle' was:

> an attempt to ensure that two sets of people [ministers and permanent secretaries] with different motivations, unable to influence each other's promotion prospects, worked together on everything of importance, to ensure enough truth and objectivity for minister's decisions, policies and bills to be as open and carefully explained as to make their underlying reasoning, and the evidence for it, reasonably transparent and clear.[1]

Foster's remedy for present ills is an appeal to establishment conscience. He does not tell us what could fire the radicalism that would defeat the power to govern badly in the hands of today's political class—unless persuaded to cede it by the obvious rightness of his fourteen pillars. It will not be easy to counter the influence of the 'placemen' interests of members of parliament or to bring into focus the diversity of the public interest in politics—where it has not been rendered apathetic by government incompetence or infantilised by state largesse.

'Tradition' could also be represented by a principle that Viscount Haldane never precisely formulated when his formidable intellect dominated political life in the first two decades of the twentieth century—but that shines out of all he did, especially in the 'Haldane Report'.[2] The principle was that there should be *formal and statutory recognition of the value of unhurried and connected forethought in government department business.* 'Thinking' was never a word to embarrass Haldane

—or the statistician A.L. Bowley when in 1919 he pressed for a Central Thinking Office of Statistics to correct the imperfections of official statistics. But move on nearly 100 years and an element of embarrassment can be detected in the advice cabinet secretary Sir Gus O'Donnell has given to public service leaders at a National School of Government conference: 'Get out and see the frontline and learn from them what is going on—don't just sit behind a desk and think.'[3]

That two political parties have, over four decades, subverted the Haldanian principle is what calls for present remedy. The principle is now under attack by the Treasury in an extraordinarily circuitous fashion—by facile demonstration that the still widely revered Haldane never explicitly subscribed to the idea that the work of Research Councils should be kept at 'arm's length' from government departments.

The Treasury does history

As chancellor, Gordon Brown asked venture capitalist Sir David Cooksey to think about how to administer the competing interests of the Medical Research Council and DoH in a single fund for health research. Cooksey's team of three civil servants was led by an economist—a senior policy adviser at the Treasury. In taking evidence, the team must have been challenged with some regurgitation of the 'arm's length' principle—as if it had been minted by Haldane. Their report[4] correctly inferred that Haldane could never have been the minter—with a quotation from the Haldane Report of 1918:

> ...many Departments must retain under their own control a distinctive organisation for the prosecution of specific forms of research.[5]

The team interpreted that as consistent with current arrangements where government departments, including DoH, commission research to address their needs. They also noted that Haldane had simply proposed the broadening of the Department of Scientific and Industrial Research he had founded, to be a *Department* of Intelligence and Research (DIR) ranking fourth after Treasury, Defence and Foreign Affairs, to deal with any problem that may require protracted research. According to the Treasury team, this shows that the establishment of Research Councils to conduct 'arm's length' research was clearly 'a step beyond that recommended by Haldane'. They take no account of the fact that DIR was stillborn and that Haldane could not have foreseen the damaging power of our modernised machinery.

The Cooksey team found their *coup de grace* for arm's length science in what Haldane had said about the Medical Research Committee ('MRC') constituted in 1911 two years before the formation of the Medical Research Council itself. Haldane had praised both 'MRC' (for the wide scope of the research that it funded) and the controlling minister (for not abusing his control). Moreover, 'MRC' had to have its research plans approved by the minister, its members were appointed by the minister and it had been supported for investigations dictated by war-time departmental needs. With that, the Treasury's defence of the idea that all types of research should depend on ministerial approval appeared to be complete. We are, however, entitled to pose a supplementary question. If ministerial appointment of committee memberships proves the dependence to which the Cooksey team was so keen to ascribe historical authority, what value can there be in the repeated claims by DoH for the 'independence' of ACRA?

The Cooksey team went on to look at the Rothschild Report. In 1971, the polymath Victor Rothschild had the ear of Margaret Thatcher, then Secretary of State for Education and Science in the Heath Government. The rest, as they say, is history—with which we are still coping! The Rothschild Report pulled no punches with a presciently Thatcherite sentiment:

> However distinguished, intelligent and practical scientists may be, they cannot be so well qualified to decide what the needs of the nation are, and their priorities, as those responsible for ensuring that those needs are met.[6]

From that judgement came the famous or infamous *customer-contractor principle* for applied research commissioned by government departments: 'The customer says what he wants; the contractor does it (if he can); and the customer pays.' LSE Professor Francis Terry has given an account[7] of the dire effects of the Rothschild principle on UK transport research and policy-making over the succeeding three decades.

The science that Rothschild had in mind was probably the hard sort, but his principle was extended to cover the soft. The Cooksey team looked at the application of the principle by DoH and noted that, from the outset, DoH struggled with its role as an informed customer and ultimately lacked the authority and experience to implement the principle for health research. They even quoted the well-targeted observations of Kogan & Henkel[8] that the Rothschild principle:

> ... failed to note how in those areas of policy where data are diffuse, and analyses most likely to be strongly influenced by value preferences, problems must be identified collaboratively between policy-maker and scientist. It failed to acknowledge that policy-makers have to work hard to identify problems, to specify research that might help solve them, and to receive and use the results of research.

The Cooksey team ended on another down-beat note that accurately echoes the many voices of discontent about the PCT-funding formula:

> ... a rigorous, integrated arrangement for the balanced allocation of resources across health research, one that could appropriately marry the needs of the NHS with the promises offered by basic science, remained elusive.[9]

These revealing comments on the history of the coordination of research are hardly consistent with the preceding defence of dependence of Research Council contracts on ministerial whim. But the inconsistency is welcome because it brings the authority of the Treasury to the questioning of the current state of affairs that motivated this book.

6

'Doing Policy': Policy-making As It Is

Radical changes may be needed to remedy the dire state of governmental policy-making, for both policies in general and policies with statistical consequences of the kind illustrated and analysed in earlier sections. For that, we need a market-place of ideas in which contributions are welcome from all those who have a strong desire for better government. For my own part, coming from a different angle and a narrower base, I am keen to know whether the (now largely moribund) statistical thinking that Haldane had recognised as a vital element of good government can be revived within the broader framework of scientific 'forethought' that is also in desperate need of revival.

The survey research reported in a recent book[1] by two academic observers of government throws light on that question. Edward Page and Bill Jenkins were allowed to interview civil servants involved in policy-making in 13 government departments. 'Doing policy' was how the middle-ranking civil servants interviewed by Page and Jenkins (P & J) would respond to the simple question 'What do you do?'. According to P & J, there are thousands and possibly tens of thousands of civil servants involved in making policy in a significant way. Should that news alarm the nation? P & J think not, for they can report that:

> Our findings suggest that middle-ranking civil servants are open to thinking in a 'joined-up' way and, together with the observation that these officials spend considerable effort trying to follow ministerial initiatives, that any problems of narrow or 'silo mentalities' have at least as much to do with ministerial or [senior

> civil service] approaches to other departments as to any shortcomings in middle-ranking officials.[2]

The interviewers' account of their findings is a subtle analysis, cognisant of the risk of biases of one sort or another. Their book has the ring of truth. The theoretical framework in which P & J interpret their findings comes from a German sociologist's defence of bureaucracy—the Weberian concept of hierarchy versus expertise *within* a bureaucracy. The tension they have in mind is between those at the top of the civil service pyramid and those half-way down—whose job is to represent or improvise the expertise needed for policy-making. The book successfully demolishes the myth that it is a matter of those at the top (pre-eminently minister and permanent secretary) having a clear idea of what they want and then getting the mechanicians lower down to give it a legal or administratable formulation. P & J expose the paradox in the pyramid metaphor:

> Broadly speaking, a bureaucracy is a hierarchical organisation; yet the activity of policymaking, which generally requires the mobilisation of specialisation and expertise, is inherently non-hierarchical. [So] how can expertise be brought to bear within a hierarchical system in which commands can only come legitimately from the top?[3]

In all of that, the term 'expertise' has to be heavily qualified. Moving up a grade in the civil service is not helped by being labelled as a genuine expert in anything. The emphasis is on 'generalist' skills. Their acquisition is aided by a mobility within and between departments that does not usually go with genuine expertise (that a department may come to depend on) but rather with improvised expertise. P & J are emphatic about that:

> [In the UK national government policy process] expertise is *not subject-based or technical*. ... The significance of this observation ... is that by minimising the impact of technical expertise on the

> bureaucratic policy process, the challenge to hierarchical authority is reduced.[4]

The expertise has to be improvised by the generalist with the occasional encouraging or discouraging 'steer' or 'invited authority' from the top. However:

> This improvised expertise poses problems for the quality of the technical advice that ministers can expect ... Highlighting obvious and public shortcomings as exposed through major scandals and blunders cannot address this.[5]

P & J give a vivid illustration of the quality problem (with strong resonance for the last of our six cases):

> An official charged with helping restructure the system of grants to local government ... suggested that 'ministers do not give a detailed steer on things at the beginning of the process'. Officials knew that the new system ... should be 'simpler and fairer', yet these goals were rather vague and conflicting since simpler formulae may not necessarily be fairer. One pointed to somewhat clearer objectives for one part of the formula:
>
> *'The key brief on the fire formula came right from the top (from the DPM [Deputy Prime Minister] if not above) to remove a well-known perverse incentive in the formula. The old formula was based on the number of fire calls ... But we want fire authorities to reduce the number of calls, false alarms, etc.'*
>
> Yet saying what the new formula should not include left open the question of what it should.[6]

So keeping things in-house, with improvised expertise and invited authority from the top, cannot ensure quality. But it is the surest way of 'minimising the impact of technical expertise on the bureaucratic policy process' and hence 'the challenge to hierarchical authority'. While P & J acknowledge the 'dysfunctional characteristics' of that way of doing things, they are willing to weigh the negatives against the fact that it addresses 'the conflict between hierarchy and expertise found in all bureaucracies'. They see the in-house practices as a harmonious solution to the Weberian problem of tension. They see it as a 'representative bureaucracy' analogous to the EU administrative system and not at all as an undemocratic conspiracy against the public interest. One constitution lawyer's review of the Page & Jenkins book does not venture to allege such conspiracy but he is critical about the consequences of dysfunctionality :

> This book helps us understand how policy ... is made; the lack of substantive expertise of many of those involved, their concern with process, and the way that major considerations ... may fail to be picked up fully by government. [7]

The pyramid that P & J have described has an architectural feature that may explain the reviewer's unease. It appears to be without windows and doors—not even a tunnel except to other government departments. That cannot be the reality; the pyramid cannot be the hermetic structure that P & J's description of what its inmates do with their days brings to mind. A truer metaphor of a government department would indeed lack the windows through which the public at large might see what goes on but, as the privileged access given to P & J itself demonstrates, it would have doors. However, those doors are down the side or at the back, where they discreetly admit the consultants and advisers who are every day playing an important role in the on-going secretive policy-making.

7

Policy-making As It Could Be

Avenues of reform

Few reforms get under way without a head of steam—in the heads of a large *enough* section of society, or group of individuals who want *enough,* and are informed *enough,* to do something about it. Realistic expectation of action by any particular section of society will depend on whether those three enoughs are enough to get things moving, which has to mean giving coherent support to some sort of small-p political programme.

Two overlapping tribes are, at least, informed enough to be influential in our cause: university researchers and statisticians. What hope is there of effective action? University staff are now stretched on the rack of current government policies for higher education. The wheel of the rack is revolved, in turn, by the Higher Education Funding Council, the Quality Assurance Agency and the executives of the Research Assessment Exercise—the notorious RAE started in 1986 under Thatcher that in 2008 gave universities their sixth work-out. These taskmasters and their agents in university administrations provide an over-stimulating environment in which wider scandals (especially those that bring financial benefits) only manage to engage the fitful attention of isolated academics. Statisticians might achieve something by working through the Royal Statistical Society but expectations must be tempered by two factors. The large overlap of RSS membership with university staff brings to bear again the adverse factors in that sector. The second large overlap is with civil servants in the Government

Statistical Service, which brings insider knowledge but also an understandable reluctance to press issues forcefully.

Fortunately, there is another currently active channel of hope. Following the public policy disasters of recent decades, there is an increasing number of 'the great and the good' who are keen to give the present state of affairs more than fitful attention. Sir Christopher Foster has drawn together a dozen such individuals into an organising committee for his Better Government Initiative (BGI). All but one are former-this or former-that—from jobs in and around government that may have seeded their support for Foster. BGI has made recommendations that could one day motivate specific proposals for the reform of contractual departmental policy-making machinery.

Reconstruction

Reconstruction rather than revolution may allow the necessary changes to be made in an evolutionary and ameliorative framework. If enough political will could be generated, these could be achieved within a short period by well-considered application of Haldanian principle. The first two recommendations of the BGI paper *Governing Well*[1] are:

R1: The capacity of Parliament to scrutinise the proposals of the Executive and to hold it to account for its decisions should be strengthened. Parliament should provide for more rigorous initial analysis of policy proposals ...

R2: Before policy decisions are taken by the Government, proposals should be thoroughly tested by objective analysis ... and by wider consultation.[2]

Haldane had foreseen the need for the first recommendation: that the increasing activity of departments would require increased power in the legislature to check the acts and proposals of the executive. The BGI people are probably thinking of grander policy-making than construction of a technique for measuring police force productivity, a safety camera partnership programme or funding formulae for the NHS or local government. Nevertheless, their recommendations will have to apply with as much force to such projects, given their huge financial significance. Our concern here is with such projects, and that is where what BGI has to say about departmental expertise becomes particularly relevant.

As Page & Jenkins discovered, the within-departmental conception of 'expertise' is that it is an improvised *ad hoc* skilfulness of those civil service generalists who are required to handle matters that in fact call for something different—a genuine expertise, either technical or specialist. Francis Terry's observation on the concept of 'generalism' is second-hand but telling:

> One of the most telling observations by the Transport Commissioner for London, Bob Kiley, on his early meetings at the Treasury was to find the room filled with economists, special advisers, lawyers, 'generalist' civil servants and—'Not a [transport] operator among them'.[3]

Not generalist but specialist is what the BGI's *Governing Well* conceived expertise to be. The introduction to their 40th recommendation could not be clearer in what it expects from civil servants:

> The capacity of Departments to construct well-designed policies through the use of thorough, structured consultation and expert research and analysis has been eroded and needs to be restored. Departments with a policy development function should be *centres of excellence* in their field, with a *strong technical capacity of their own* and strong links to academics and practitioners outside government and to overseas experts...[4]

Another BGI paper, *Government Departments,*[5] raises even further the bar that departments should be able to jump:

> Policy development in many areas of government is a highly specialised evidence-based activity. To carry it out successfully a Department needs ... professional staff whose expertise *at least matches that of outside institutions* [and] who are able to understand and *pass objective judgement* on the various scientific, technical and other expert material relevant to its activities. (p. 9) [Emphasis added.]

For the civil servants who write Cabinet papers, BGI's *Governing Well* raises the bar even higher:

> Some green and white papers deal with matters that involve detailed technical, scientific, economic, statistical or other expert analysis that is not accessible to non-specialists. They must nevertheless be expressed in terms that enable the *complete argument* to be followed by *non-expert Parliamentarians and members of the public*. (p. 15) [Emphasis added.]

It is doubtful whether the new machinery for that could be up and running in less than a decade, even if attention were first paid to the kind of expertise required for the soft science necessary for policy-making. The following modest proposals may be realisable in shorter time, during which their success could be a stimulus to progress of the grander project. The proposals are drawn from an outsider's analysis of current practice. They do not depend on changes in personnel, other than a crucial willingness of existing staff of all grades to adopt new ways of administering the contractual machinery. They therefore relate to policy-making for which a department lacks some essential expertise.

The present practice appears to be as follows. For whatever reason—Cabinet direction, ministerial whim or internal inspiration—a department finds that it is facing a policy-making problem or project too complex for within-departmental resolution. Once the decision is taken to put the problem out to contract, six wheels in the contractual machinery have to be turned, in succession:

1. The department has to specify the project in broad enough terms to be accommodated in a press advertisement or in a web-site notice requesting an Expression of Interest.
2. The department has to send the Expression of Interest notice to individuals or groups that it thinks may have a particular and informed interest.
3. The department has to specify the project, and the then-perceived options for proceeding with it, in enough detail for the advertised Invitation to Tender to elicit informed responses.
4. The department has to decide which individuals or groups are personally invited to tender.
5. The department has to decide whether any of the tenders it receives in response should be taken seriously and, if so, which of the tenders is the winner.
6. The department has to decide, in its further work on the project, whether to make use of any portion of the final report of work from the winner.

The individual tenders, including the winning one, remain confidential. The publication of the final report appears to be at the discretion of the department. At all stages, the department may get advice from a confidential advisory committee or 'steering group' that may then be described as 'independent'—for no other reason than that its membership is made public. It would be a contribution to hindsight wisdom to get the full details (chapter & verse and numbers) of the choices and decisions in the turning of the six wheels in a sample of failed projects. A cross-cutting inter-departmental committee of specialists and generalists with an admixture of parliamentarians and outsiders should then be encouraged to ratiocinate free of political pressures.

The cumulative record suggests that project failure can easily be seeded in one or more of the six administrative stages, especially if civil servants are too sensitive to the wishes of their political masters. There is, moreover, the unresolved paradox that a department that has already conceded that it lacks the competence to resolve the technical problems in the project (even when aided by an advisory board or steering group) is expected to get things right—to make the right choices and decisions—at all stages of the procedure. It is the expectation that contractual machinery alone can be used to process scientific uncertainty that needs to be questioned.

In conclusion, here are six suggestions for how to reconstruct or recondition the machinery:

1. Consult widely in the early stages of an uncertain project. Solicit the views of separately active individuals or groups likely to have divergent opinions (e.g. economists and statisticians) well before any attempt is made to specify an invitation to tender.[6] At this stage, discord may be highly informative which the later competitive tendering arrangements (financially valuable contracts) could not reasonably be expected to be.

2. Be prepared to extract the informative value of any discordant opinions from those thus solicited. Discord is a likely outcome when the realities of any complex issue are searchingly addressed. For cases where the disagreement is between two well-argued and persuasive approaches and where the costs of outside expertise are small compared with the financial risk of a misguided policy or defective formula, be prepared to back competing research teams.[7]

3. Enlarge Haldane's legacy by restoring the pre-1960s balance between economists and statisticians in order to get greater prominence for the statistical-thinking component of forethought.

4. Use publication to curtail the ministerial practice of claiming confidentiality for advice received from advisory committees that the minister claims to be 'independent'.

5. Publish on paper or web-site all advice obtained from external consultation, whether paid for or not.

6. Publish the winning tender along with the departmental reasoning for its acceptance.

England has enough civil service talent to effect a step change in the quality of policy-making. In other words, the generalists' grey matter can do it, provided they can shake off their ministerial incubus. We need not wait for departments to become Foster's 'centres of excellence'—a transition that might well have to await changes in our genetic pool. In the short run, the important genes are not those that enhance intelligence but those deeper atavistic ones from our simian origins that feed social Darwinian behaviour i.e. survival of the fittest. A simple change in the definition of 'fittest' would work wonders for policy-making: the fittest civil servants would be rewarded for employing their endowed intelligence in accordance with the high standards inscribed on Sir Christopher Foster's fourteen pillars. That change can only come about when Parliament asserts its authority to determine the framework in which the 'public interest'—which is nothing more than defence of the citizenry against the arrogance of a ruling class—can be guaranteed.

Playful Postscript

In the 1870s, Norway was in a political ferment, trying to throw off the Swedish yoke. Literary giant Bjørnstjerne Bjørnson was inciting students with a call to 'Live in Truth!'. His play *Det Ny System*[1] (*The New System*) transferred that call to those who were condoning corruption of the Norwegian state in the shadow of Swedish rule. In 1913, his English translator wrote:

> In these days, when the best men all over the civilised world seem agreed that the most effective remedy for social evils and mistakes lies in publicity, The New System has a timeliness almost equalling that of a political platform.

It is a drama whose timeliness has not faded, but Bjørnson never explains what the 'new system' is. All the audience is told is that it has to do with the engineering design of the railway system of a small country. The mother-in-law of one engineer gives us a clue when she expresses her contempt for his 'figures and wheel diameters; figures and curves; figures and track-width, friction, deadweight—ugh!'. It seems that the country's canal inspector (CI) has a guilty secret: years earlier he had enthusiastically praised the new system so highly in a number of foreign periodicals that it became the railway engineering system imported into the country. A whistle blower (WB) eventually exposes the system as an 'expensive, a disastrous mistake, which it would be a crime to disregard any longer and that is costing the country millions'.

For years the new system has been administered by the CI's brother-in-law—the director-general (DG) of railroads—who also has a guilty secret. To protect the family honour when he got to know about an engineering flaw in the system, DG faked the figures in a table of 'weight of rails, driving-wheel momentum, dead weight, wheel diameter' when he addressed a railroad congress in Paris so that the flaw would remain hidden. The play's leit-motif is WB's effort to get CI and DG to make public confession of their secrets and thereby 'live in truth!'. Only with CI is he successful. The DG finds another way of living with the truth in a dialogue with his chief clerk, Larssen, who comes on stage to disturb DG's soliloquy. In their face-to-face dialogue, Larssen reveals that he has faith in the system only because he has trusted DG's own faith in it!

LARSSEN: *Didn't I believe? Of course, I believed!*

DG: *The deuce you did! You only believed in me.*

LARSSEN: *... Yes, one of us has been fooled. That new system of yours—*

DG: *Mine? It isn't mine!*

LARSSEN: *Whose can it be, if not yours?*

DG: *It was in practical use long before me.*

LARSSEN: *And yet it was you who introduced it?*

DG: *I? Am I the government? ... Have I the power to introduce anything?*

LARSSEN: *... all the same—Why!, it was done by the Commissions, of which you—*

DG: *Do you think I appointed the Commissions? Or that they were made up of me alone?*

LARSSEN: *Well—this is the end of it! ... And yet ...* **the estimates** *were misleading.* (Bjørnson's emphasis)

DG: *That's too bad! For the estimates were made by you Larssen—by yourself and the rest of the office.*

DG refuses CI's advice to confess before deciding to spend more time with his family.

Bjørnson gave his characters other lines with a strikingly contemporary resonance:

CI TO WB: ... *the engineers in this country are like all the rest. Either they* have *public employment or they are looking for it. And if they are doing private work, then they either* have *made a success of it or they want to do so—and in neither case do they care to quarrel with those in power ... the big truths that might lead to an explosion—they are not told.* (Bjørnson's emphasis)

DG'S SON (reading WB's exposure of the flaw):

... he goes on cold-bloodedly—oh, so coldbloodedly and so logically—to figure out how much the country loses by it annually. And it ends up with some beautiful reflections about the moral effect on our engineers. For they are now compelled to stand by what at bottom they don't believe in, and this becomes possible only by means of calculations and data held to be far from legitimate.

DG TO HIS WIFE:

Life is so far from being based on truth that, instead, all its fundamental relations are based on a tacit agreement never to let the whole truth out. To be more truthful than custom demands is nonsensical, unmannerly, stupid perhaps even dangerous.

CI TO WB: *I don't mean that the stupidities are to be preserved for all eternity. All I mean is that we shouldn't delve too much into everything, and thereby make the trouble still worse. It comes out all right in the end, if only we give it time.*

CHAIRMAN OF RAILROAD COMMITTEE:

> *... it isn't easy for the Diet [the country's parliament] to decide as long as the experts remain divided among themselves.*

WB'S ENGINEER FATHER (driven to drink by his battle with the system):

> *The Diet? What does the cat know about mustard? Are those who sit in it engineers, do you think? Chatter-boxes, that's what they are. ... Why should we engineers get angry? What's the use of having a state, if it doesn't pay for our stupidities?*

Notes

Introduction

1 The pyramids get a name-change from time to time but they can weather storms as well as the Egyptian ones do.

2 See Page, E. and Jenkins, B., *Policy Bureaucracy: Government with a cast of thousands*, Oxford: Oxford University Press, 2005.

3 *Computer Weekly*, 18 September 2007, p. 12.

4 See Fairtlough, G., *The Three Ways of Getting Things Done: Hierarchy, Heterarchy and Responsible Autonomy in Organisations*, Axminster: Triarchy Press Ltd, 2007; and Seddon, J., *Systems Thinking in the Public Sector*, Axminster: Triarchy Press Ltd, 2008.

5 Now that a philosopher has been appointed chairman of the UK Statistics Authority perhaps the list should be extended to embrace thinkers who can leaven the professional dough.

6 Gleick, J., *Genius: Richard Feynman and modern physics*, London: Abacus, 1994, p. 428.

7 For the 10-year projection of net immigration from the accession in 2004 of eight East European countries to the EU, ministers initially presented the economists' confidence interval, 5,000 to 13,000, as if it was for the short term.

8 Gilbert, W.S., 'My Dream', in *Bab Ballads*, London: Macmillan, 1908.

9 Stowe, Harriet Beecher, *Uncle Tom's Cabin*, Boston: John P. Jewett & Co., 1852, Chapter 20.

1: Kill or Cure by Formula in a Statistical Playground

1 Department of Health, press release, 11 December 2002.

2 Hawkes, N., 'Time to face up to "scandal" of funding formula: The government is in denial about the effects of funding inequities on primary care trust deficits', *British Medical Journal*, Vol. 334, 2007, p. 395.

3 The curly brackets { } are not the ones you find on a pocket calculator—they turn whatever expression they embrace into a national index.

4 The bits of the formula in bold and italic type hold a dark secret—to be revealed in the next-but-one section.

5 Department of Health, *A Brief History of Resource Allocation in the NHS 1948-98* (RAWP 4), London: Department of Health.

6 Department of Health, *Resource Allocation: Weighted Capitation Formula,* London: Department of Health, 2003.

7 Department of Health, *Resource Allocation Exposition Books,* London: Department of Health, 2003.

8 *Hansard,* Written Answer, London: House of Commons, 20 July 2006.

9 *Hansard,* Written Answer, 20 July 2006, p. 1.

10 *Hansard,* Written Answer, 20 July 2006, p. 103.

11 Civitas Lunchtime Discussion, 'Equality and Choice in Education', 19 July 2007.

12 Stevens, S.L., 'On the lost art of analysis', *Health Service Journal,* 29 March, 2007, p. 15.

13 *Hansard,* Written Answer, London: House of Commons, 8 January 2003.

14 Sutton, M. *et al, Allocation of resources to English areas: individual and small area determinants of morbidity and use of health care resources,* NHS Scotland's 'AREA' report and DoH's RARP 26, 2002.

15 Gravelle, H. *et al,* 'Modelling supply and demand influences on the use of health care: implications for deriving a needs-based capitation formula', *Health Economics,* Vol. 12, 2003, p. 985.

16 Stone, M. and Galbraith, J., 'How not to fund hospital and community health services in England', *J. R. Statist. Soc. A (Statistics in Society),* Vol. 169, 2006, p. 143.

17 This reformulation has been made for the years 2009 to 2011. See Morris, S., Carr-Hill, R., Dixon, P., Law, M., Rice, N., Sutton, M. and Vallejo-Torres, L., *Combining Age-related and Additional Needs (CARAN) Report,* RARP 30, London: Department of Health, 2009.

18 Smith, P., Rice, N. and Carr-Hill, R., 'Capitation funding in the public sector', *J. R. Statist. Soc. A,* Vol. 164, 2001, p. 217.

19 Smith, P., *Formula Funding of Public Services*, London: Routledge, 2007.

20 House of Commons Health Committee, *NHS Deficits, First Report of Session 2006-07*, Vol. I, London: The Stationery Office Ltd, p. 24.

21 Sutton, M. *et al*, *Allocation of resources to English areas: individual and small area determinants of morbidity and use of health care resources*, NHS Scotland's 'AREA' report and DoH's RARP 26, 2002, p. 166.

22 The Office of National Statistics concedes that there are large uncertainties in its estimates.

23 Darzi, Sir Ara, *Healthcare for London: A Framework for Action*, London: NHS, 2007.

24 Darzi, *Healthcare for London*, 2007, p. 19. [Emphasis added.]

25 Darzi, *Healthcare for London*, 2007, p. 20. [Emphasis added.]

26 In *The American Economic Review*, Vol. 73, 1983, p. 31.

27 In *The American Economic Review*, Vol. 73, 1983, p. 31.

28 McCormick, *Explaining NHS Deficits, 2003/04-2005/06*, 2007, pp. 6 and 98. [Emphasis added.]

29 McCormick, *Explaining NHS Deficits, 2003/04-2005/06*, 2007, p. 59. [Emphasis added.]

30 E.g. to favour either deprivation or age, depending on what would be the right thing to do.

31 House of Commons Health Committee, *NHS Deficits, First Report of Session 2006-07*, Vol. II, London: The Stationery Office Ltd., pp. 61, 62.

32 Asthana, S., Gibson, A., Moon, G., Dicker, J. and Brigham, P., 'The pursuit of equity in NHS resource allocation: should morbidity replace utilisation as the basis for setting health care capitations?', *Social Science & Medicine*, Vol. 58, 2004, p. 539.

33 House of Commons Health Committee, *NHS Deficits, Sixth Report of Session 2005-06*, Vol. II, London: The Stationery Office Ltd.

34 *NHS Deficits, First Report of Session 2006-07*, Vol. 1, p. 81.

35 *NHS Deficits, First Report of Session 2006-07*, Vol. 1, p. 81.

36 *NHS Deficits, First Report of Session 2006-07,* Vol. 1, p. 81.

37 Morris *et al, Combining Age-related and Additional Needs (CARAN) Report,* RARP 30, 2009.

2: Water Under the Bridge or Lessons to be Learned?

1 Bevan, R.G., *Review of the Weighted Capitation Formula (RARP 33),* London: Department of Health, 2009, p. 4.

2 Phrases such as 'state of the art' and 'sophisticated statistical methods'.

3 Bevan, *Review of the Weighted Capitation Formula (RARP 33),* p. 8.

4 Bevan, *Review of the Weighted Capitation Formula (RARP 33),* p. 76.

5 O'Hagan, A. *et al,* 'Subjective modelling and Bayes linear estimation in the UK water industry', *Applied Statistics,* Vol. 41, 1992, p. 563.

6 *Metro* (Business), 18 April 2008, p. 55.

7 Spottiswoode, C., *Improving police performance: A new approach to measuring police efficiency,* Public Services Productivity Panel, 2000; Available at www.hm-treasury.gov.uk/pspp/index.html.

8 Two critiques surfaced in 2002 in *Public Money and Management,* Vol. 22, p. 33, and *Statistics in Society (Journal Royal Statististical Society Series A)* , Vol. 165, p. 405.

9 Public Services Productivity Panel, M*eeting the Challenge,* London: The Treasury, 2000, p. 12.

10 A City law and accountancy firm that, according to Simon Jenkins, was recorded in 2005 as consultant on 174 government projects with a capital value of £31.4 B.

11 The Royal Statistical Society's oversight of the PwC report had been requested by the Association of Police Authorities.

12 'Efficiency or deficiency', *RSS News,* Section Reports, September 2000, p. 19.

13 For Linda Mountain's outspoken article 'Safety cameras: stealth tax or life-savers?', *Significance,* Vol. 3, 2006, p. 111.

14 Hooke, A. *et al*, *Cost Benefit Analysis of Traffic Light and Speed Cameras,* Police Research Series Paper 20, London: Home Office Police Research Group.

15 Stone, M. , 'Adjudication of the Radio 4 *Today* Programme Speed Tribunal', *Research Report 245,* London: UCL Department of Statistical Science, 2005.

16 The Consulting Group and UCL, *The National Safety Camera Programme: Four-year evaluation report,* London: Department of Transport, 2005.

17 Dustmann, C., *The Impact of EU Enlargement on Migration Flows,* Home Office On-line Report 25/03, London: Research Development and Statistics Directorate, 2003.

18 House of Commons Select Committee on Home Affairs & European Scutiny, 7 December 2006, Q. 52.

19 House of Lords Select Committee on Economic Affairs, 23 October 2007, p. 38.

20 *Research Report 235,* London: UCL Department of Statistical Science, 2003.

3: Breaking the National Silence

1 Benveniste, G., *The Politics of Expertise,* London: Croom Helm, 1972, pp. viii-ix.

2 'Evanomics—Figuring out real life: Migration intricacies'. Available in 2008 at: bbc.co.uk/blogs/thereporters/evandavis/2007/03/migration.

3 BBC *Today* programme interview with Phil Collins and Tim Harford on July 25, 2008.

4 'Official statistics, public policy and public trust', *J. R. Statist. Soc.* A, Vol. 171, 2008, p. 1

4: Breaching Whitehall Confidentiality

1 Gainsborough, S., 'Surplus-rich PCTs anxious of cuts in new allocations', *Health Service Journal,* 29 November 2007, p. 5.

2 House of Commons Health Committee, *NHS Deficits, First Report of Session 2006-07*, Vol. II, London: The Stationery Office Ltd.

3 *Hansard*, House of Commons, 19 December 2005.

4 House of Commons Health Committee, *NHS Deficits, First Report of Session 2006-07*, Vol. II, London: The Stationery Office Ltd.

5 Woodhouse, D., *In Pursuit of Good Administration: Ministers, Civil Servants, and Judges*, Oxford: Clarendon Press, 1997, p. 153.

6 ACRA also stands for Aluminium Can Recycling Association, which clearly serves the public interest.

7 Foster, Sir Christopher, *British Government in Crisis: The third English revolution*, Oxford: Hart Publishing, 2005, p. 298.

5: A Lost Battle of Lords?

1 Foster, Sir Christopher, *British Government in Crisis: The third English revolution*, Oxford: Hart Publishing, 2005, p. 222.

2 Haldane Report, *Report of the Machinery of Government Committee*, London: Ministry of Reconstruction, 1918.

3 O'Donnell, G., 'Lessons to be learned from the frontline', *Public Servant*, December 2007, p. 8.

4 Devenish, P., Austin, A. and Connolly, J., [The Cooksey team], *Historical Overview of Government Health Research Policy*, London: H.M.Treasury. Available at: hm-treasury.gov.uk/media/6/B/cooksey_review_background_paper a_brief_history.pdf.

5 Haldane Report, *Report of the Machinery of Government Committee*, p. 32.

6 Appendix 'The organisation and management of Government R & D', to *A Framework for Government Research and Development*, London: Stationery Office, 1971, p. 4.

7 Terry, F., 'Beyond predict and provide', in Davies, H.T.O., Nutley, S.M. and Smith, P.C. (eds), *What Works? Evidence-based Policy and Practice in Public Services*, Bristol: The Policy Press, 2000.

8 Kogan, M. and Henkel, M., *Government and Research: The Rothschild Experiment in a Government Department*, London: Heinemann, 1983, p. 9.

9 Devenish *et al*, *Historical Overview of Government Health Research Policy*, p. 13.

6: 'Doing Policy': Policy-making As It Is

1 Page, E. and Jenkins, B., *Policy Bureaucracy: Government with a cast of thousands*, Oxford: Oxford University Press, 2005.

2 Page and Jenkins, *Policy Bureaucracy*, p. 146.

3 Page and Jenkins, *Policy Bureaucracy*, pp. 10, 13.

4 Page and Jenkins, *Policy Bureaucracy*, pp. 147, 148.

5 Page and Jenkins, *Policy Bureaucracy*, pp. 165, 167.

6 Page and Jenkins, *Policy Bureaucracy*, p. 84.

7 Trench, Alan, *Modern Law Review*, Vol. 70, 2008, p. 872.

7: Policy-making As It Could Be

1 BGI, *Governing Well* is available at: http://www.bettergovernmentinitiative.co.uk/sitedata/Misc/Governing-Well.pdf

2 BGI, *Governing Well*, p. 2.

3 Terry, F., 'Reforming the public services', *Further and Higher Education Newsletter*, No. 12, Spring 2006, p. 9.

4 BGI, *Governing Well*, pp. 9-10. [Emphasis added.]

5 BGI, *Government Departments* is available at: http://www.bettergovernmentinitiative.co.uk/sitedata/misc/BGI-Report-on-departments---rev-25-Nov.pdf

6 A lighter 'brain-storming' might be useful. In the early stages of any forethought, experts should be kept apart to maximise their independence, their number should be greatly enlarged and individually motivated to offer a disinterested opinion by, for example, a contribution to their organisation's tea-club.

7 The idea had a grander scale for Maynard Keynes :

'It will be remembered that the seventy translators of the Septuagint were shut up in seventy separate rooms with the Hebrew text and brought out with them, when they emerged, seventy identical translations. Would the same miracle have been vouchsafed if seventy multiple correlators were shut up with the same statistical material?' from *Economics Journal*, Vol. 50, 1940, p. 154.

Would that that had been done for two groups of health economists in the early Nineties!

Playful Postscript

1 Translated by E. Bjørkman as *The New System*, London: Duckworth & Co, 1913.